THE 7
SECRETS
TO
CHANGE
YOUR CAREER

THE 7 SECRETS TO CHANGE YOUR CAREER

Escape Your Prison and
Build a Dream Life

PAUL COPE

ISBN: 978-1-5272-3529-8

First published 2019

Copyright © 2019 Paul Cope

CONTENTS

1

WHY I CAN HELP

Does your job make you unhappy? Do you ever feel as though you're living the wrong life? Do you think you were destined for better things?

I know how it feels to be stuck in a place where you feel unfulfilled and alone. I also know how it feels to go from that place to a different world. A world filled with hope and excitement. Most importantly of all, I know how to guide you from where you are now to where you want to be. I've walked the path, battled through the darkness and defeated the demons, and I've created a map to show you the way to travel so that you can avoid the pain that I suffered along the way.

If you're anything like me, though, as soon as you start reading something like this you'll have a healthy cynicism about the author and what he can possibly teach you. Given the world we live in, you're right to be cynical.

So, it's important to set the scene for you and to explain why I'm certain that if you feel stuck in your career, this book is everything you've been looking for and will give you the practical, psychological and emotional tools needed to release yourself from the prison you've built around you.

It all goes back to my origins story, which is a bit like those X-Men movies but instead of getting bones made of steel, or the ability to shoot laser beams from my eyes, I got a career that made me miserable.

It wasn't the super power I dreamed of as a little boy, if I'm honest.

*   *   *

I'm sitting in the back of a white Nissan Datsun with a steering wheel in front of me. He's sitting in the front with his own wheel. He looks a bit like the ex-manager of Arsenal Football Club, Arsene Wenger, but with shorter hair. He's my hero. He knows everything. We're driving along on a beautiful sunny day with clear blue skies and I'm looking out of the window at the world passing by. We stop at traffic lights and a black Porsche pulls up next to us.

"Whose is that?" I ask in awe at the shiny sports car.

"It's our solicitor's" he replies.

"I want to be a solicitor then."

*   *   *

And that was that.

I was three years old and sitting in the back of my dad's car. Depending on your age you might not remember a time when kids sitting in the back seats of cars didn't have smart phones and tablets to keep them occupied, but in 1983 the equivalent of an iPhone driving game was a plastic steering wheel that you stuck to the window with a rubber sucker. Remember them? I used to love sitting there, pretending to drive along behind my dad. I loved cars. I had hundreds of toy ones that I kept in a big white bucket in my wardrobe and played with every day, so seeing that black Porsche for the first time had me absolutely mesmerised.

When I heard that it was a solicitor who had that car, that was that. Well, as far as I know that was that. I don't actually remember it. The scene I describe to you is the one in my mind from all of the times I heard the story growing up. A story planting a seed, one told by my elders over and over until I started telling it to myself and others. I was certain throughout my school life that I wanted to be a solicitor, with the comedy value of the anecdote being that I couldn't even pronounce the word properly when I was three (I was a slow learner in the talking department, which might be why I'm trying to make up for it now).

You might have known a kid like me in school; someone who everyone else envied because they knew exactly what they wanted to be. While pretty much everyone else around me questioned what he or she might end up doing on a daily basis, I had it all planned out.

Weirdly, there was nothing about my day to day school life that indicated I'd want to sit in an office all day reading case law and drafting documents, other than the fact I was pretty bright and getting good grades.

More than anything I was an artist as a kid; an artist and an entrepreneur. During class and break times, I used to draw pictures of the Teenage Mutant Hero Turtles (they weren't allowed to be called 'ninjas' in the UK because it was apparently too violent for us), then sell them to class mates for 20 pence each. The demand came before the supply – probably my best ever business.

When I got older a few mates and I used to knock on the doors of neighbours and ask if we could wash their cars, charging £3 per vehicle. A lady once offered us the choice of £3 or a jar full of two pence coins and I recall quickly estimating how many coins were in there and taking the chance. I don't remember if it ended up being more or less than £3, but the risk-taking entrepreneur was in me even back then.

No one identified the potential businessman or nurtured the artist in me, but I went through my school life quite happy. I worked hard and ended up getting the A-Levels I needed to go to university to do a law degree. There were a few little blips on the way, most notably while I was in the middle of working on my art GCSE in the lead up to deciding what A-levels to study. A class mate asked if I would continue to study art at a higher level. Mr Power, my dark-haired, bearded art teacher was profound in his reply.

"Of course he is" he said.

"Sorry sir, but I can't. I've asked the university and they said they won't accept art as a real A-Level so I'm going to do an extra maths subject instead."

That's my first real memory of starting to betray the inner me. It was the first time I'd been forced to choose between who I really was at my core and who the world wanted me to be.

I can still remember the look on Mr Power's face now. He must have encountered that problem time after time. Thinking back, quite a few of the best artists in the class were also good students, already destined to become doctors, dentists and lawyers and turning their backs on their creative side. I wonder where they are now and how their lives have worked out.

The first real turning point in my life, though, came aged 19 when I was in the middle of my law degree. It was the second year of a three-year course and a big national law firm was giving a presentation on how to get a job with a company like theirs, which was the dream of most in the room.

*   *   *

We're sitting in an old-fashioned tutorial room typical of red-brick universities in England. The desks are dark and at least 30 years old, probably more like 50. The light is dim and the air is cold and musty, but I can feel the anticipation from all of the young, hungry law students waiting to hear how they can fulfil their dreams at a top corporate law firm.

I'm wearing a full track suit, sporting a shaved head and have gold jewellery dripping from my wrists and neck (one of my many misguided looks over the years), eagerly awaiting the guidance of the young sage lawyer standing before me.

"When you come for an interview" he says, *"you'll be asked why you want to be a solicitor."*

"I've got this covered" I think to myself. *"I've known since before I can remember."*

"There's only one answer that will not be accepted under any circumstances."

The pause feels like it goes on for an eternity as the fresh-faced junior solicitor leaves us all hanging for dramatic effect.

*"You can't say that you've always wanted to be one. It's a cop out and we need to know **why** you've always wanted to."*

Smack. Right across the middle of my overly pronounced nose. I feel like I've been hit by a bat in the face. My head starts spinning and 16 years of life start flashing before my eyes.

"But, I have always wanted to be one … I don't know why, I just have."

* * *

Looking back, the fact that the young lawyer even made that point during his presentation indicated that there were probably thousands of kids like me, inadvertently prodded down the road of being a lawyer by the sophisticated mind-bending experts known as 1980s parents, who I'm certain were the inspiration for the 2010 movie *Inception* with Leonardo DiCaprio. Maybe you were one of those kids, prompted to be a lawyer, a doctor, a dentist, a nurse, an engineer, a mum or a plumber by the people you spent the early stages of your life believing had all the answers.

Tell me you don't believe in mind control and I'll show you as many examples of families corrupting their youth as you can handle. It's all well intentioned, obviously, but I still can't really comprehend why any parent thinks they have the right to decide what their child does with their life, or to *"guide"* them along the way. But that's a topic for another book altogether.

Back to 1999, and I was in disarray. Having been so certain that I wanted to be a solicitor for almost my entire life, I now realised that the whole thing was based on a story about a car at traffic lights. I don't even know why my mum and dad would have had a solicitor when the origins story was set, so it could all very well have been bollocks from the start.

But that didn't help me halfway through a law degree.

I remember not knowing what to do and thinking about changing direction before too many years were lost. Then I went out for a drink with my family and had a chat with one of my favourite uncles, one that I'll never forget.

* * *

We're sitting in a little old pub in Anfield, a suburb of my home city, Liverpool, not far from Liverpool Football Club's home stadium. Holy ground as far as I'm concerned. The walls are painted red and adorned with multiple images of footballers and photos from the good old days when the world was a simpler place. The air is thick with the cigarette smoke pouring out of every second punter in there, and the light is struggling to break through the tiny windows overlooking the main road to the front. We're sitting just past the long bar on the right as you walk in, huddled in a corner away from the hustle and bustle.

"What would you want to do with your life if you could do anything you wanted, son?" he asks.

"I'd play for Liverpool Football Club".

"And what are the chances of that?"

As his words ring in my ears, I look down at my 19 year-old rotund frame, all fat not muscle, mainly caused by my heavy drinking in university and my love of burgers and pizza, and glance at my dodgy knees and pint of lager in hand, and say:

"Slim to none".

"The thing is son, nobody likes their jobs. Most people hate them. If it was meant to be fun they wouldn't call it work. So, if you're not going to be a footballer you might as well do something that makes loads of money."

To the ears of a naive teenager it sounded pretty logical, and I was sold. I decided there and then to continue with my degree and make the most of it. I'd be a rich lawyer after all, and nobody enjoys their job, do they, so why should I be any different? At least I'd get to drive that sports car.

I ploughed on, achieving the degree I needed by the skin of my teeth and going on to qualify at one of the biggest corporate law firms in the world at the time, which was also by far the biggest and most prestigious in my home city.

At first the job was great. I worked with amazingly talented people, made countless friends who I'm still fortunate enough to call mates today, worked long hours and partied like it was 2005 to 2008 (granted, it doesn't have a great ring to it but they were the actual years so I'm not going to lie just for the sake of poetry).

It wasn't long, though, before I started to become disillusioned with it all. Seemingly arbitrary rules, nonsensical ways of dealing with clients that served only to piss them off, and a culture that treated employees like cattle, each starting with shiny eyes and fire in their bellies, before realising that they would easily be replaced by the next young buck on the conveyor belt if they didn't play ball.

A friend and colleague in our first year as trainee solicitors was told in her first six-month review that while the firm was delighted with her work, the partners thought she should spend more time in the office to just show her face a bit more.

When she questioned why she needed to stay longer than necessary if all of her work was done, they couldn't give her anymore of an answer than, *"well that's just what we do around here"*.

I should have known then it was never going to get any better, but I lasted two years before jumping ship to a major rival to see whether all big law firms were the same, knowing in my gut that they were thanks to the stories I'd heard from friends at similar companies.

Despite the new firm being equally impressive, professional and packed with amazing people, it only took me a few months to realise that it was basically the same as the first company and no doubt all other law firms (and big corporations) around the world.

I was frustrated. I was earning £45,000 per year and billing at least five times that for the firm. I was brilliant at networking and winning clients, but every client or new job I brought in just meant that I had to work longer hours for the same amount of money. From a purely financial perspective it made no sense to me.

A friend and I calculated our hourly rate by dividing our annual salary by the number of hours we were working and realised that we were being paid about the same as we would if we were painting houses for a living, but without the ability to listen to a radio and do gentle exercise all day.

It didn't sit well with me but I wasn't sure what to do. After all, I'd spent my whole life working towards this point. My family was proud of me, I was earning good money and I knew there were decent promotion prospects if I continued to work my arse off for the next 10 years. I also fitted in with my friends who did pretty standard jobs working hard for a fixed salary.

Are you in that position now, or something similar?

I was confused. Part of me felt like I was valued in my role, but another part of me remembered in my previous job watching one senior partner after another leave to a fanfare only for the company to carry on the next day as if they had never been there. No one, it seemed, was as valued as they thought.

For years I listened to people saying they couldn't quit their jobs because they couldn't let their colleagues and friends down, then they'd eventually leave after things got too bad to live with and no one gave a shit anyway.

All those wasted years.

I thought through each of the reasons for staying and decided that none of them were valid. My family was proud, but they loved me so surely they'd be happy as long as I was happy? And anyone who was a real friend would back me no matter what.

Then I looked at my salary and started breaking things down. I asked myself the simple question of whether I backed myself to earn the minimum amount I needed to survive each month if I left a secure income behind.

As I considered it all, I looked at the things I'd achieved in life up to that point. All of the exams passed, the degree, the qualification as a lawyer, and I realised that I was capable of doing anything that I put my mind to. I calculated that I needed £2,000 a month to cover my fixed expenses and that I'd only need a few small clients each month to cover that.

I wanted to be in charge of my own destiny, not earn money for a big business that didn't value me. I also knew that while there were promotion prospects within law firms, if I stayed I'd never be in control of how much money I could earn or when I'd be promoted, if ever.

At that point I decided to go it alone. I'd identified a niche in the market that no one else was targeting and set up my own boutique law firm. Everyone told me I was brave, but I could see in their eyes that they meant stupid. I was giving up a secure, well-paid job with great promotion prospects to forge my own path, and it felt electrifying.

The day I left my last 'normal job' I felt like an inmate in a prison movie who had just climbed over the perimeter fence and was running for freedom, with my old jailbird friends cheering me on from inside the walls, hoping I'd make it just to give them some hope.

Cope & Co solicitors was born in September 2009, a day after I was officially permitted to set up my own practice by the Law Society of England and Wales. Starting with a baby face, chubby cheeks, a pen, a blank piece of paper, a phone and Google, I built a real company. A law firm with offices and clients, like a proper grown up would do.

I was so pleased with myself.

Then I started to grow it, to run before I could walk, to make mistakes. I hired people with no idea how to be an employer or any idea of how to build a functioning culture. I was learning it all as I went along, discovering more in a few years than in a lifetime before.

Over time, though, it became less and less fun. It became harder to get out of bed every morning and easier to make excuses to avoid the office. I was the managing director and the main fee earner. I was well and truly working in the business, not on it, and was quickly starting to drown under the gallons of water pouring into a vessel I'd constructed. Sleep was becoming a rarity and cash flow problems becoming a new monthly visitor I could have done without.

I was burning out at a rate of knots.

Before that point in my life I had been one of those smug bastards who when people asked how old I was, I'd confidently come back with the immortal line *"how old do you think I am?"*, knowing that they'd guess anywhere between five and 10 years younger than my real age. I know, I could punch myself in the face thinking about it.

Around that time, though, I started getting guesses of *"I don't know, 40-odd?"*.

I was 32.

Not only were things not working out as well financially as I'd hoped, I was also depressed. Not on medication, or diagnosed clinically, but ticking every box on the *"are you depressed"* checklist of NHS online. I was struggling to get out of bed, hating going into the office I'd built and not recognising the person looking back at me in the mirror every day, or the lad barking at people and generally being miserable.

Leading up to that point I'd experienced various moments which, in hindsight, were the universe trying to tell me something, but I obviously wasn't ready to listen back then.

Something had to change, and the first turning point was Christmas night 2012. I got married that year and spent tens of thousands of pounds on a luxury wedding in a hotel fit for Premier League footballers in Mallorca, Spain.

But that was only after having nearly killed myself running my law firm while completing a property development in my 'spare' time to pay for it all. (Obviously the best thing to do while stressed out of your mind running your first company is to take on the development of a derelict, burnt out three-storey property with no roof, it's what all of the healthy living guides recommend.)

Christmas was celebrated at my mum and dad's house, which meant that after the festivities I was left lying in the bed that I'd spent my childhood years in, staring at the ceiling with my new wife asleep next me, struggling with the insomnia that had haunted me for years.

The walls and ceiling were all white, with a blue carpet and the same bed and furniture I had grown up with: light brown wardrobes and a chest of drawers nestling either side of a double bed, with hardly any room to move. On the wall facing the bed to the right-hand side of a large window was a painting of a footballer, Duncan Ferguson, that I'd produced when I was 16 during my art GCSE course.

All around me were mementos of another life. It was like being suspended in a time capsule surrounded by memories of how things could have been; a different universe where I'd gone on to be an artist or to do something else I loved.

I started flicking through my phone and I came across a book called *The 4-Hour Work Week* by Tim Ferriss, which caught my attention because a mate had recommended *The 4-Hour Body* by the same author to me a few months earlier. I had dipped in and out of it but had never read it properly.

I downloaded a sample and started reading.

And kept reading.

Since that night I've always believed the maxim *"when the student is ready, the teacher appears"* and, as it turned out, I was ready for Tim Ferriss to be my teacher and the principles in his book to be my new guiding lights. I ordered the full paperback copy and took it on my honeymoon with me a week later to read on the beach.

People often laugh at this stage of the story and say that they can't believe I was reading a business book on my honeymoon, so let me make clear what I tell everyone else: **I wasn't reading the book out loud.**

My new wife didn't care whether I was reading a business masterclass or Harry Potter.

That book was the start of a journey that led, years later, to me writing and you reading this. I remember lying on a sun bed on the beach devouring the pages. The sky was bright blue with a few wispy white clouds drifting by, the air was still and it was scorching hot to the extent that the hotel employed people to walk around spraying cool water on guests.

I went through the book and immediately starting redesigning my new life on a piece of paper. I began thinking of all of the ways I could streamline my company to make it more bearable to run, as well as having an entirely different epiphany. I suddenly realised that the only reason I had a law firm was because I was already a lawyer and I wanted to start my own business.

But what if I was starting again from scratch? What if I could start with a blank piece of paper and a pen and design a completely new business with no restrictions? And that's when I started to get excited.

Think about it for a second. What would you do tomorrow if you could start again from scratch and redesign everything? What would your life look like? What would you be doing every day to make yourself happy?

I sketched out how things would look, but rather than start with an idea and working forwards, I started with what my life would look like at the end and worked backwards.

Having realised I would need hundreds of employees to grow a law firm to the place I dreamed of being from a wealth perspective, and having recently seen Instagram sell for $1billion with a team of 13 people, I decided that I wanted an online business that could scale quickly with a small team. I wanted something recession proof in an industry that I had an interest in, and for it to be fun every day.

By the time I'd finished I had a list of the constituent parts of my perfect business and began joining the dots to decide what industries fitted the bill.

The result was online gambling.

I'd always been a big football fan and enjoyed a bet, and I knew people loved to have something to help distract from their daily lives at weekends. I realised it would be pointless trying to compete with the industry big boys so, just like with the law firm, I found a niche that wasn't being filled and started designing an idea.

When I got back from my honeymoon I was absolutely on fire. I started putting in place systems within my firm to alleviate stress while I was working late into every night and over weekends on building a new business in a completely alien industry, learning from scratch how to get a gambling licence in the same way that I'd figured out how to open a law firm.

There were problems even at that phase, and I quickly realised that principles you read about in books filled with tools and techniques are all well and good, but the real world doesn't always act in a way consistent with what we might hope for.

Doing things like setting up email autoresponders to deal with people trying to contact me did nothing other than rub them up the wrong way, while trying to get employees to jump on board with new ideas that I thought were brilliant – but were completely alien to the industry they'd worked in – created a ridiculous amount of emotional problems that I just wasn't equipped to handle.

On top of that, I was building another business in the background that distracted me from work with my main company.

It all meant that the period between January 2013 and January 2016 was nothing short of a rollercoaster. I had a huge number of incredible highs and crushing lows along the way, including disputes within the law firm, securing a big private equity investment in the gambling business, working with my wife for two years and, ultimately, a big crash.

It was stressful enough running the law firm without building another enterprise alongside it, and the stress only increased when the online business went from a relatively small operation during evenings and weekends in its first year to scaling rapidly after I'd secured investment.

I decided to sell my law firm in 2015 in order to focus fully on the new company, which I thought was my *4-Hour Work Week* road to riches, but it all quickly turned sour.

Just when it looked as though we were ready to break into the stratosphere with an exciting new marketing partnership, a big competitor copied my online gambling concept and we had a web development catastrophe that brought everything crashing down.

It completely destroyed me and by the end of 2016 I realised I was absolutely ruined, financially, psychologically and emotionally. I was completely out of gas.

It was like what happens to rechargeable batteries. At the start they work perfectly, then you run them down, charge them back up and go again. But after a couple of charges they stop getting back up to 100 per cent no matter how long you charge them for. After a while, a charge only lasts for a few hours and, before too long, they won't recharge at all and just need to be thrown away.

I was at the point where the batteries just needed to be thrown away.

Even holidays didn't recharge anything, usually because they just involved continuing the work and stress from the setting of a different country in a different time zone rather than actually having a break.

I was depressed, sad and the powerful mojo I used to feel inside every day had disappeared. I was dragging myself through life using hundreds of techniques I'd learned and read about from various mentors in various books and podcasts over the years. Those tools and tricks enabled me to function and keep a facade up to the world that was needed for survival, but that was all they achieved: survival.

I was still doing consultancy work for the law firm I'd sold my business to at that point, which meant that I had enough income to survive, and I decided to spend a few months taking some time out and taking better care of myself. The doughnut, pizza and Jack Daniels diet I'd been propping myself up on for years is not one I've seen advertised in many places and not one I'd recommend if you want to stay alive past 40. I knew it was time to reassess everything.

Then, after a few months of rest and recuperation, an offer came along. I was introduced to a contact of a contact who wanted to speak to me about a job. They were launching a new gambling company run by a team of experts with a fresh approach to the industry, and they thought I'd be a good fit.

I'm always open to conversations about new opportunities so I went along after some initial talks by phone and ended up having a really interesting meeting with two of the senior people in the business. I explained what I'd done in the past and they remarked how unusual it was for someone to have my background, which was a perfect match with what they were doing.

They went away and came back with an offer to be their head of legal for Europe with a bumper salary, the opportunities to receive shares in the business and to be awarded significant pay rises as the company grew.

I can't say I wasn't tempted.

I discussed it with my wife and family. I could sense they wanted me to take it. They would have been happier for me to call time on my dream of living a happy and fulfilling life away from the day-to-day drudgery of a standard 9 until 6 existence working for 'the man'.

I could feel myself being pulled between the two worlds. Between a place I'd dreamed of being for years and the old world I'd been a part of for so long; a world I knew made me unhappy. I'd been there for over a decade, working away for other people, never completely satisfied, always wondering if there was something better out there.

I turned the offer down. I went with my dream and with my heart. It caused some trouble at home and led to a little personal criticism from outside, but that didn't matter. The people who love and support me didn't judge, they just wanted me to be happy. The people who did judge me, didn't matter.

That was over 12 months ago, and I couldn't be happier to tell you that it was the right decision. After going through that experience, it forced me to reflect on everything I'd done in life up to that point. I thought about everything I'd learned, the ups and downs and years of struggle. I remembered the many books, podcasts and courses consumed in order to develop in two totally different industries (as well as developing properties on top of it all).

I realised that I'd made so many mistakes that I could have avoided had I been able to turn to someone to guide me during those early days of changing careers.

Then I realised that I could help other people. I thought back to being a little boy and looking after the new kids who joined the class, which seemed to be a role that the teachers unofficially appointed me to, and it dawned on me that what makes me happy in life is helping other people and inspiring them to live better lives.

And now I had a map to show them how to do it.

I set up a new venture and started working with business owners to help them, using my experience to solve problems in their companies, and helping them to remove the things in their lives that were causing them sleepless nights.

Only now I wasn't just using tips I'd read in a book, I was showing them how to implement things in real life and how to avoid the mental and emotional pitfalls that I'd experienced during my toughest years.

It worked. Clients loved what I did and it really helped them. I could see in their faces how much my experience and my input was doing to improve the quality of their lives, so I started mentoring people to help them to do the same and start taking steps to move away from jobs that were making them miserable.

Which brings us to where I am now, free of the stress, pain and suffering that was once a daily companion. More importantly, I've achieved much more than I ever planned during that journey. What I thought was an adventure to earn more money and work for myself has led to a complete transformation in my life.

I've realised that since those days as a little boy, when I first heard that story about the Porsche and began telling myself that I wanted to be a lawyer, I'd slowly been turning my back on the real me: the little kid who loved to draw, take care of people and try new things.

I'd allowed myself to become an angry, tense, miserable shadow of my true self: a man whose ego was running wild and whose life had started to fall apart.

It's only through this wild odyssey that I've been able to do something much greater than change careers. I've been able to rediscover myself and transform my life.

In addition to all of that, my health had been deteriorating since I was 17. Auto-immune diseases took a grip, manifesting themselves in Crohn's disease and a degenerative illness going by the overly complicated name ankylosing spondylitis.

The latter caused my neck to practically stop working and my joints to ache every day. For over 10 years I suffered with an incredible pain deep inside my right shoulder that just would not go away no matter what I did.

But now it's gone.

A year after finding the path that was right for me a physical pain that plagued me for over a decade just disappeared. I know it sounds crazy, I'd think it was too if it hadn't happened to me, but it has. My neck is slowly starting to get better and I believe that within a few months I'll be free of any symptoms of Crohn's.

I'd be lying if I said that I've managed to conquer all of my demons. I haven't, and I don't expect them to ever go away completely. But I have come to accept the ones that remain as part of the ebb and flow of normal life. I have reached a place where my day-to-day life is peaceful and content, my health is improving on a daily basis and I can spend plenty of time each day going to the gym and walking my dog while listening to podcasts and audiobooks.

What all that means for you is that whether you want to quit your job to work for yourself, join another company to improve your quality of life, become a gardener or sell ornamental piglets online for the rest of your time on this planet, I can help you get there.

There are books I've read that help you to figure out what to do next or how practically to change what you're doing, but what I haven't found yet is a book that gives you tools and techniques and takes you through the mental and emotional blocks that are getting in your way, stopping you living the life you want and having the career you've always dreamed of.

That's why I've written this.

I believe that we can all live a happy and fulfilling life. My mission now is to help as many people as I can to do just that, giving you the confidence to make bold decisions, inspiring you to change your life for the better and showing the mistakes I made along the way so that you can avoid making the same ones.

I've learned that life is simple but not easy. Whether you want a six pack instead of a beer belly, more money to spend on shoes you'll only ever wear once or a fulfilling career, the principles are simple.

But simple and easy aren't necessarily the same thing.

You want to lose weight? Simple. Just eat fewer calories than you burn every day. Easy? My sugar and chocolate addictions say otherwise. I know how to get a six pack, I just really struggle to do it.

I once heard the great marketer and author Seth Godin say that certain things in life are self-regulating, six packs being one of them. Only the people completely dedicated to getting one will ultimately succeed in the long term. You can cheat and get surgery, but it won't last when you're still shovelling chocolate bars into your mouth every day (that bit is mainly directed at me, not you).

The same rules apply to changing your career to something more fulfilling. It can take time, patience and commitment, but I'm here to take you step by step down the path to having a job that makes you forget what day it is instead of being something you have to drag yourself to every Monday morning, counting down the hours to Friday afternoon before the dread restarts again a few hours later.

If you feel that you're wasting your life, that you were meant to do more than you are right now and you believe that you deserve better, then come with me. I will take you on an adventure that helps you to realise all of the ways in which you're standing in your own way of making the changes you want to make. You can demolish the obstacles in your path and build an incredible new career and a new life.

Just allow yourself to drift off for a few seconds to that place you dream of; the life you always thought you'd have that has become inextricably linked to the hope of a lottery win that never comes.

What does it look like? How does it feel? What can you hear? Just sit and think about it.

I bet it's calm and peaceful, or fast and exhilarating. Or a bit of both. I bet you wake up every day feeling happy and full of energy. You sing in the shower and can't wait to start your day, bringing joy to all of those you meet and spreading love and happiness to everyone close to you. Your money worries have disappeared and you no longer have to answer to an idiot boss who hasn't got a clue.

You can take off for a few days holiday whenever the mood takes you and treat yourself to those little gifts that you deserve for all of your hard work. Just thinking about it makes your shoulders relax, the stress lift and your breathing slow down.

I promise that all of those things are possible. I know, because I've done it.

And the best bit is the part that almost stopped me from writing this. The self-doubt that we all experience that often stands in our way affects me as much as it affects you. A few months ago, I was asking myself *"Who am I to write this? Why should you listen to me?"* I'm not rich, I'm not famous and I'm not a millionaire.

But then it dawned on me: that's exactly why I should write this now, because it will never be more powerful than at this very moment.

I don't know about you, but whenever I hear a multi-millionaire telling me all the ways that we can change our lives, I hear a little voice in my head telling me that it's okay for them. While I know that they might have started out like the rest of us at some point, once they've become rich and famous some part of their message becomes lost on some of us.

Hopefully writing this book at this stage of my life will help it to resonate more with you than any book by any multi-millionaire or TV superstar.

I'm a normal lad earning a good income having transformed my life from a corporate slave working 100 hours a week, ruining my health, personal relationships and peace of mind, to that of a generally relaxed, happy and content person working 25 hours a month and enjoying spending time walking my dog, reading books and looking after myself properly, while rebuilding relationships that were so badly damaged by my previous life.

I promise that if you decide to buy this book and follow the step-by-step process, by the end you will have an actionable plan that you can follow setting out how to break free of the prison you've found yourself in and stroll, shoulders back, head up into the life you've always dreamed of.

The most important point is that this is no ordinary non-fiction book. This is not just an instruction manual about implementing strategies and getting a new job. This is a book about magic. A book about hopes and dreams and wish machines. This is a book that will take you back to when you were a little kid, with nothing but a thriving imagination about all of the possibilities in the world. To a time before bills and bosses, to a world before settling for *just okay*, to a land before everyone else convinced you that grown-ups aren't meant to have fun every day.

I believe that life was meant to be more than that. I believe with every fibre of my soul that you can have more than everyone else tells you. I believe it because I've lived a life for everyone else and I've lived a life outside the structure that they all wanted me to live, and I can tell you that living your own life is much more fun, peaceful and enjoyable. Living with a smile on your face and joy in your heart, able to let the weight of the world fall off your shoulders and the grief and grime of daily life drift past you like a gentle breeze. It feels incredible.

I believe that you deserve more than you currently have, and I believe with all of my heart that you are capable of more than you think. I've realised that my role on this planet is to help as many people as I can to live a happy and fulfilling life, and I'd love you to allow me to guide you along the path.

It is all possible. You just need to believe that it is.

JANUARY 2019

All things
are
possible
for those
who
believe

2

SHOULD YOU BUY THIS BOOK?

I appreciate that it's probably unusual for an author to give away free chapters at the start of his own book telling some people not to buy his work, but I don't like being like everyone else and we're all weird in our own way, aren't we?

So, here's the thing.

Why you shouldn't buy this book

I don't want you to buy this book if it's just going to sit on a shelf at home or, worse, tucked away in a drawer, never to be read. I don't want it to turn into something you resent buying or something that's sitting on your ever-increasing list of things that you think you *should* do, slowly making you feel worse about yourself on a daily basis, a little piece at a time.

That isn't good for me and it most definitely isn't good for you. I want this book to be a source of positivity in your life, not something else adding to the negativity. I'm sure you've already got enough of that to deal with.

I only want you to buy this book if you are ready right now to take steps to change your career and have reached that point where you're so fed up that you're ready to do what it takes to transform your life.

There are a number of ways you can check if you're ready, but here's my favourite one.

Imagine a scale from zero to 10, where zero is that you would do absolutely anything to change from where you are right now. Zero is you crawling over hot coals, telling your boss to go fuck himself or herself and skipping out of your workplace without looking back, running for the hills swirling your jacket over your head.

Ten is being absolutely satisfied where you are, with not a care in the world and happily bouncing into work every day with all of your clothes in the right place.

What number would you give yourself? Don't think about it, just let whatever number popped into your mind be the answer. Your gut reaction is your best guide here, before your brain gets involved and convinces you that your gut is wrong.

Have you got the number? Great. Now here's the kicker.

You can't have seven.

Seven is a cop out. Seven is the number we use when picking out of 10 to avoid things either being slightly bad or slightly good. Seven is 'meh'. Seven is what people mean when they describe something as vanilla, even though vanilla is actually an amazing flavour so they should really be using something bland like flour or dust to make the point.

In fact, whether or not you decide to buy this book, please do me a favour and next time someone describes something bland as 'vanilla', punch them in the face and shout "YOU MEAN IT'S LIKE DUST – VANILLA IS FUCKING LOVELY."[1]

As soon as seven is removed as an option you have to decide whether you're more an eight or a six, which is when things become real.

So, if you picked seven, are you more a six or more an eight?

If you're an eight or higher, I'd suggest that you probably don't need this book. It may be that where you currently are is actually where you're happy to be, which means that you're unlikely to take the steps necessary to change things if they'd mean you experiencing even a small amount of pain in the process.

I'd suggest you think about your current role, writing down all of the ways in which you like or even love it, and all of the ways it pisses you off. Then consider how you can remove the things that annoy you and enhance the things you like. Just focusing on the good bits is likely to make you happier and more satisfied with what you have.

I was talking to someone at the end of a wedding a few months ago who spent the first half an hour of our conversation saying nothing but negative things about her job. I was a bit drunk and in a bad mood, so decided to challenge what she was saying and asked why she didn't leave if she was so unhappy, instead of nodding along politely as I might ordinarily do.

---

[1]   Please don't actually do this, it's just a joke.

Her response was that she loved her job.

Given how surprised I was by her answer, I asked what percentage satisfaction she'd give herself (a slight variation of the above test), and she said 70%.

Having gone through the process about 70 per cent not being allowed, without getting anywhere, I pointed out that if she really was 70 per cent happy in her job, she could transform her entire life by choosing to focus on the 70 per cent of her work that was positive instead of the 30 per cent that was negative.

The same might well apply to you and, if it does, this principle applies to everything else in your life as well and can transform your outlook on the world overnight.

In short, if you are happy about something that everyone else thinks you're miserable about, you need to have a word with your face.

If that does apply to you but you'd still like to buy this and see the keys to unlocking a happier life and a more fulfilling career, just bear in mind that none of the ideas or tools set out in the book work in real life without you taking action.

You can't get a six pack just by reading about how to do it, you actually have to eat less Ben and Jerry's ice cream and do more exercise (another note for me together with a hope that this book sells loads of copies and Ben and Jerry's ends up asking me to be the face of their company).

Why you should buy this book

If you gave yourself a six or below then you're well and truly ready to buy this book and will probably get through this whole guide in the next few days, taking action immediately, tearing down walls and bursting into your new life.

If that is the case I'm excited for you to get started. If I could go back now and speak to my younger self, teaching him the lessons I've learnt and helping him to avoid the pain he was destined for, I'd love to do it. Luckily for you I can't do that because, if I could, we'd be left in that weird time loop that happens in *Terminator*, where it doesn't really make any sense because if I could go back in time and help that little lad, then I'd never have been so miserable and would never have written this in the first place. Just like John Connor.

Anyway, 80s film-time-loop references aside, the fact that I can help you to change your life makes me so happy and helps me to fulfil my own passion so, from an entirely selfless perspective, always remember that by reading this and taking the steps necessary to change your life you're also helping another human to fulfil their own passion. Perfect karma in itself.

As you've seen from my origins story in chapter one, I've been accumulating lessons for 38 years, including for the past 10 years the most intense crash course in business and life that I could never have paid for anywhere in the world (and I'm pretty sure if you could pay for it, it would be closed down as an inhumane business venture). The lessons in this book are the culmination of all of the pain I've endured throughout that time and, most importantly, are there to make sure that you don't experience the same pain. I share my experiences and help others to avoid the bear traps along the way because I know that if I had found the right mentor when I was changing careers, I wouldn't have made a fraction of the mistakes I ended up making.

I am fortunate enough to have the ability to aggregate complex information and disseminate it in simple to understand ways. When I was running my law firm, I once took on a job for clients who were in the middle of a large business sale and sacked their lawyers because they were useless. They asked me to join a meeting and told me that we had two weeks to complete because they'd already wasted six months with the previous firm. I sat down, went through the detail with everyone, boiled it all down to its simplest form and walked everyone to completion on schedule. The accountants involved afterwards commented that they'd never seen anyone assimilate such a complex deal so quickly and simplify it so well.

I don't tell you that to brag (well, maybe just a bit), but to point out that it looks like the super power I got was the ability to learn and to listen to loads of things and summarise them to other people in easy to understand ways, adding my own interpretation to make sure that the principles work in the real world.

Granted, it's still not flying or seeing through walls and Hollywood isn't going to make a movie about me any time soon, but it's a lot better than the miserable career I thought I'd got as my super power in my origins story, and means that I can actually help people in ways lots of other people can't.

If you read this and are thinking that you already have that super power, I've put a list at the end of this chapter of all of the key books I've read over the years as well as all of the podcasts I've listened to and key blogs I've read. It's impossible for me to list all of the thousands of articles I've read, videos I've watched, experiences I've had or courses I've been to, but at least it will give you the basic building blocks if you'd rather go your own way and do this yourself. If you do decide to do that, you do so with my best wishes and no hard feelings. It's more important to me that you are true to yourself and go your own way than it is that you buy this book. It also gives me an opportunity to acknowledge and thank all of the many amazing people from whom I've learnt over the years from afar.

If you do decide to choose me as your guide for this expedition, when you get to the end of the book you will see that I've included my personal email address for you to contact me with any questions about anything you're stuck on, frustrated with or with which you just need a bit more guidance. As well as happily receiving your questions, I'd love you to let me know when you use the tools and techniques that are set out in the following chapters to release yourself from your current life and catapult you into a new, happier and exhilarating future. Good news stories are always nice to hear.

To ensure that I deliver on my side, if you buy this book and don't find value in it, I'll personally refund the price you paid if you return the book within 30 days of purchase. That's how certain I am that the secrets contained in the following pages will change your life. I can't say fairer than that.

If you do decide to come along with me, there is one secret to change your career contained in the next chapters that I consider to be the single greatest secret you will need to uncover in order to move forward.

Whether or not you come along, though, I wish you all the health, happiness and success you've ever dreamed of.

If you are joining me on the quest for a better career and life, I'll see you on the other side.

The 7 **SECRETS** To Change Your Career

Surrender & Take Responsibility

Essence

Count the Numbers

Rationalisation & Excuses

Ecstasy

Taking First Steps

Secret of Secrets

Books, Podcasts and Mentors

Here is a list of the key books I've read and podcasts I've listened to, in case you want to delve into the detail of any of the sources of some of my knowledge or do your own reading without having to buy this book. At least, it's everything that I can remember at this point in time. There are countless individual articles and blogs I've read, videos I've watched and lessons I've learned over the years which have helped me along the way, but which have long since been lost to the world of the back of my mind despite my best efforts to remember them all.

I can never thank the various legends and superstars listed on the next page enough for the guidance that they have given me from afar.

Books

Awaken the Giant Within (Tony Robbins)
Blink (Malcolm Gladwell)
Bounce (Mathew Syed)
Cash Flow Quadrant (Robert Kiyosaki)
Crushing It (Gary Vaynerchuk)
E-Myth Revisited (Michael Gerber)
Expert Secrets (Russell Brunson)
Factfulness (Hans Rosling)
Find Your Why (Simon Sinek)
Freakonomics (Stephen Levitt/Steven Dubner)
Hooked (Nir Eyal)
How to Think and Grow Rich (Napoleon Hill)
Influence (Robert B Cialdini)
Mindsight (Dan Siegel)
Man's Search for Meaning (Viktor Frankl)
Outliers (Malcolm Gladwell)
Principles (Ray Dalio)
Recovery (Russell Brand)
Rules of Management (Richard Templar)
Start with Why (Simon Sinek)
Super Freakonomics (Stephen Levitt/Steven Dubner)
Surely you must be joking Mr Feynman (Richard Feynman)
The 4 Hour Work Week (Tim Ferriss)
The 4 Hour Body (Tim Ferriss)
The 4 Hour Chef (Tim Ferriss)
The 22 Immutable Laws of Marketing (Al Ries and Jack Trout)
The $100 Start Up (Chris Guillebeau)
The Alchemist (Paulo Coelho)
The Monk who Sold his Ferrari (Robin Sharma)
The Power of Vulnerability (Brené Brown)

The Strangest Secret (Earl Nightingale)
The Truth (Neil Strauss)
Think Like a Freak (Stephen Levitt/Steven Dubner)
The Magic of Thinking Big (David J Schwartz)
The Obstacle is the Way (Ryan Holiday)
Traction (Gabriel Weinberg and Justin Mares)
Tricks of the Mind (Derren Brown)
Vagabonding (Rolf Potts)
What I Learned Losing a Million Dollars (Jim Paul and Brendan
    Moynihan)
When to Rob a bank (Stephen Levitt/Steven Dubner)
Zero to One (Peter Thiel)

Podcasts and Blogs

Business Wars (Wondery)
Freakonomics Radio
How I Built This with Guy Raz
Masters of Scale with Reid Hoffman
Philosophize This (Stephen West)
The Gary Vee Audio Experience
The Tim Ferriss Show
The Tony Robbins Podcast
Mark Manson *(https://markmanson.net/)*
Tim Urban *(https://waitbutwhy.com/)*
Alain de Botton *(http://alaindebotton.com/)*

"If you could kick the person in the pants responsible for most of your trouble, you wouldn't sit for a month."

–THEODORE ROOSEVELT

3

SECRET 1
SURRENDER & TAKE RESPONSIBILITY

It's late at night and you can't relax because you're already dreading tomorrow.

You've been in this position for years now. You might have loved it once or vaguely remember how exciting it used to be at the start, but you don't enjoy it anymore. You already know that you won't want to get out of bed in the morning no matter how much sleep you've had. You definitely won't want to go to work. You know you'll endure your morning, using whatever tricks you've learnt over the years. You'll get to the office, possibly late, but the energy you used to have is a distant memory and you know that it shows to everyone around you, who are just the same anyway.

You'll get through the day with a cocktail of caffeine, sugar and maybe even some alcohol. The people you deal with will annoy you, even some of the ones you usually like, and you can already picture the conversations that you'll have to have that you just can't stomach anymore. You know that you'll survive another day and go to bed tomorrow night with all of the things you still need to do running around endlessly in your head, knowing that you'll have to get up again a few hours later and do it all over again. It's a cycle of never-ending misery.

You fantasise about running away and leaving it all behind but you can't because, worst of all, you feel trapped in a prison that you built around you and wonder how you ended up here.

You have the house to pay for, the car, the bills, the kids or the pets. Then you have a lifestyle to maintain, the internet, the credit cards and a list of other bills that have crept up over the years, all added to the pile in the hope that each would make you a little bit happier. They might even have succeeded for a while. Deciding to take the plunge and sign up for that TV subscription so that you could watch the football, box sets and movies at home, or committing yourself to a gym membership thinking it would motivate you to get off your lazy arse and lose some weight. But the initial positivity soon wore off and now you're just left with more outgoings that trap you in your miserable existence.

*   *   *

Does any of that sound or feel familiar? How many times when reading through it did you get that churning feeling in the pit of your stomach because it felt like your life?

I know it feels hopeless, that might even be why you've decided to buy this book. I can promise you, though, that while it can all feel desperate, it's not. The upside is that if you built the prison you can take it down and rebuild something else in its place.

You are in control of your destiny and the solutions are at your fingertips. I know all of this because I've walked in your shoes and changed everything.

Let me take you back to 2014. It's autumn time so the days are getting darker much earlier and the temperature is dropping. It's a time of the year when, if you're in the right mood, things can look pretty and peaceful, but generally it's just shit because the summer's over and it's wet, cold and dark, and you're miserable at work and grumpy at home.

I've been running my law firm since 2009 and, to the outside world, everything seems great. I'm 34 years old with a beautiful, charismatic wife, a business with a city centre office with fancy glass walls, a team of employees and a list of impressive clients good enough to grace the files of any major legal practice. I've even got a black sports car that I always dreamed of. There's just one problem with it all.

I'm absolutely fucking miserable.

I hate every day. I hate going into my own office, I hate most of my clients, I hate everything. Worst of all, I can't even bear to look at myself in the mirror. How has all of this happened? It was all meant to be so different. It was meant to be my dream but it's turned into a living nightmare. I spend my days arguing with my wife, trying my best to keep a lid on my anger, depression and frustration in order to manage my employees and deal with clients, juggling phone calls, emails, meetings and socialising with my peers having to put on a brave face every time I step into a networking event.

"How's business Paul?"

"Oh, fantastic thanks Jack – really busy but I can't complain."

"Pleased to hear it. Can I just ask about the job that Jim is working on for us? We really thought it would be finished by now. He did tell us it would be next month but we thought, you know, maybe you could push it a bit faster for us."

"OH, JUST FUCK OFF AND LEAVE ME ALONE, JACK – NONE OF THIS FUCKING MATTERS ANYWAY!"

Of course, I didn't really say that last bit. That's just what we fantasise about saying, isn't it? In reality, it was more like, *"Oh, no problem at all, Jack, let me have a chat in the office about it tomorrow and let you know. Obviously, we want to do everything we can to help".*

I'm sure if you asked my employees and my closest clients and contacts from back then what they thought they'd probably tell you they could see the seams starting to come apart.

I used to ask employees to tell me when anything was going wrong so that I could do something about it, but in hindsight my body language wasn't giving out the same message as my mouth which made sure that problems tended to stay hidden. In fairness, I'd be reluctant to tell my boss that I had a problem if they were storming around the place every day, looking worn out and depressed. It's not healthy for anyone in an organisation to feel that way, let alone the leader.

Without knowing it, I'd worked myself into the ground while becoming less and less fit and destroying my body with a terrible diet and too much alcohol, all used to numb the pain of a miserable existence sat behind a desk for 12-hour minimum days, six and seven days a week. Not a great mix.

Have you ever been in that position? Are you there now, or something close to it?

In the middle of that nightmare, something happened in the autumn of 2014 that completely changed my view of my life. It was nearly two years after I'd read *The 4-Hour Work Week* and I'd implemented a few techniques that had helped in some practical ways with day to day life, but hadn't solved the root causes of my problems.

I was lying in bed, wide awake in the early hours of the morning as I tended to be, considering all the ways in which I'd built a prison around myself. All of the debt, all of the commitments. I was blaming everyone else for everything. It was my wife's fault for not supporting me enough and my clients' fault for being too demanding. My employees were too needy and my friends and family not interested.

Sound familiar?

The main problem is that when we find ourselves in a negative place, we very rarely take a step back from the challenges we face and ask ourselves what we could have done or could do better to resolve or avoid a headache. Instead, we instinctively start blaming the people around us.

When our boss gives us a ridiculous deadline to complete a task, we create amazing new ways of insulting them inside our own heads as opposed to wondering what steps we could take to improve the situation. When an employee doesn't follow our instructions, we instantly blame them without asking ourselves whether the instructions were clear enough in the first place. When a customer repeatedly does something that is not in line with our systems, we moan internally about how stupid they are rather than questioning whether those systems could be improved to make life easier.

Even with something as simple as exchanging messages with friends, we assume that because we know what we mean when we write the message it's also clear to the person at the other end, so any subsequent confusion must be their fault.

It's all pretty common and is an issue in society as much as one in our work lives. We're almost taught to blame others by the culture we're brought up in. Why take the uncomfortable step of analysing your own behaviour when you can blame someone else? Pick any topic you like and you'll see the same principle running through its core, from that dispute you've got in the office, to the argument at home, through to sports team owners sacking managers they appointed weeks before and leaders of countries avoiding responsibility for anything and everything in order to blame something (anything) else.

But here's what I've learnt. While blaming others might give us an immediate feeling of relief or allow us to avoid a difficult conversation with ourselves, it doesn't help us in the long term. It's a bit like eating a cake because it makes us feel good for 30 seconds, while every day looking at ourselves in the mirror and feeling depressed at what we've become. It's having an alcoholic drink every day to cheer ourselves up in the short term, without realising that it's making us depressed and miserable in the long term.

While the world might teach and encourage us to point the finger at someone or something else, all that leads to is a feeling of helplessness in whatever situation we find ourselves. Blaming others for our problems inevitably means that the solution is out of our control, whereas if we take responsibility for our circumstances we can take ownership of them and make them better. Of course, there are lots of things over which we have no control that we should just do our best to ignore.

For those things that we are able to impact upon, it's time that we start asking what more we can do instead of blaming the other party.

Rather than constantly telling ourselves that we are right, we can ask ourselves how do we know that to be the case. We can challenge our beliefs by asking those around us how we can improve and asking what we are doing that's causing the very problems that we're complaining about.

I remember hearing a story a few years ago about a managing director of a company whose biggest complaint was that he received too many emails from his employees. He was bombarded every day, he said. It was only when the employees were asked that the MD realised that it was his fault. He started every day by sending emails to the entire workforce, who then felt obliged to reply for fear of looking as though they either hadn't read the email or didn't care about its content. By learning that one thing, the MD changed his own behaviours which solved his biggest bug-bear in the company overnight.

What are you doing that might be causing the stresses and strains that you're currently battling with? Rather than blaming others, what steps can you take to improve? We'll identify all of those things in the next chapter.

Having learned all of this, it suddenly dawned on me as I was lying there, wide-awake in my bed: if I built the prison myself, surely I had all of the plans I needed to take it down? If I've been the architect of my own misery, I can be the architect of a new life. Not just working around the edges trying to numb the pain, painting the walls of my jail cell or putting posters up, but ripping it down altogether.

What if I just got rid of it all?

The next day was like the first day of spring in my mind. I'd realised that by taking responsibility for everything I'd done, I could switch from acting like a helpless victim to taking control of it. I felt relieved for the first time in years.

From then everything started to change. I started figuring out all of the ways I could scale things back which ultimately led to me selling the business. Now, four years from that point my life is unrecognisable from the one I had before, so I can promise you that there is hope and you can change your current situation.

The first step is to surrender to the problems and to acknowledge they exist, which you have hopefully done before taking the step to buy this book, but it's worth discussing further.

If you have built a prison around yourself or you feel trapped, have you acknowledged yet that you were the architect of the structure from which you now want to escape? Have you taken responsibility for your situation and accepted that it was of your own making?

If not it's essential that you do before we go any further.

The most disempowering thing any of us can do in our lives is seek to claim victim status. Don't get me wrong, you may well have been a victim at some stage in your life. Something might have happened to you when you had no choice and no power to stop it, something that I wouldn't wish on anyone. Even if there wasn't any big event or big trauma, the chances are that even if you had what you always thought was a happy upbringing there are some skeletons lurking in your background that are impacting your life today.

But, whatever it was, big or small, it was in the past and does not need to control your future.

One of the biggest problems with prisons is their inhabitants can become institutionalised. I recently met a multi-millionaire who was once a guest of Her Majesty in England and, despite having put those days behind him many years ago, admitted to sometimes longing for the days when he could sit quietly in his cell reading his books and practising yoga without the noise and distractions of the outside world.

You might well have become accustomed to the prison you've built, maybe even finding comfort in the misery it brings. It wouldn't be unusual if you have. Most people who I meet on a daily basis live a life of general misery, always wishing away the days in search of Friday night, wishing away the months in pursuit of a summer holiday or Christmas, or wishing away the years telling themselves it will all be better at some future point.

The problem is that they say those things without taking any action that would lead to a change of circumstances, resulting in them being forever trapped in their life of servitude, pinning all of their hopes on the potential of a lottery win. They dream of a better life and expect it to materialise without changing any of their actions or behaviours.

Do you know anyone who does that? Anyone who drifts away to a dreamland in which they fantasise about what they'd do if they managed to pick those magic numbers?

Maybe you are that person.

The good news is that by the end of this book, you will have a plan in place that can provide you with the lifestyle you probably associate with lottery winners without the depression that often greets the people you only see on the news with their oversized cheques.

They don't usually show you what happens to people when they've spent their whole lives telling themselves a story about all of their problems being caused by a lack of money, only for the money to come along and expose the truth that money doesn't solve misery. Obviously, it's a more comfortable life having the money you need to do whatever you desire, but it's not a panacea. It doesn't solve the fact that your relationship with your partner is straining at the edges, your kids seem to be at loggerheads with you or that you often feel alone in the world. As the saying goes, quick riches are more dangerous than poverty.

The important thing for the purposes of this part of your journey is to acknowledge and accept that you are the creator of your own life. You have made a series of decisions that have led you to this very point, even to purchasing this book. You might not like some of the decisions in hindsight and you might have made them to make someone other than yourself happy, but you still made them. At every point you had the option to choose something different but, up until now, you didn't.

It's likely that there were other structures built around you that you couldn't control. A family system that you didn't design and a society you were born into that you didn't create. We can't do anything about the things we can't control, but we can choose to not let them define the things that we can change.

Today is where you take control. Today is the date in your life that you will always look back on and remember with a smile on your face. Take a moment now to note what day it is and where you are. Soak up the environment that you're sitting in because you'll need it one day when you're telling the story about the moment your life changed for the better. This will be your autumn 2014, when the world shifted on its axis and you suddenly felt empowered to change everything. When you looked around you at the walls you'd built and realised the greatest thing about having constructed your own prison is that, without knowing it, you've had the ability to tear down the walls all along.

It's important to remember as a caveat to all of this, though, that taking responsibility is not the same as beating yourself up about everything. This is not an invitation to swing from blaming everyone else to blaming yourself and tumbling into a spiral of self-pity. Instead, it is a prompt to take a reasonable, balanced view of the issues surrounding you and to analyse them in a calm and measured way, identifying the areas you can improve.

If you can find the right balance, taking responsibility for your problems will be the single biggest thing you can do to begin the journey to resolving them. It might be more uncomfortable than blaming others in the short term but, in the long run, it will improve your life and make you more content.

I will help you to find the first crack in the infrastructure of your prison and slowly, together, we'll start to rip it down piece by piece. Picture the scene in *The Shawshank Redemption* when the warden throws a hand-crafted chess piece at a poster of Raquel Welsh only to see it burst straight through, uncovering an escape hole that Andy Dufresne had been tunnelling for years.

That hole exists in your prison, you just can't see it yet. But you will.

Embrace the mistakes you've made. Admit that you are in control of your own life, the good parts and the bad, and feel the rush of empowerment flooding through your veins. You'll notice a feeling of total calm wash over you, your shoulders relaxing and your breath slowing. The knot inside your stomach and the tension in your back slowly easing.

This is just the start of your escape movie.

4

SECRET 2
ESSENCE

What are the root causes of the
things you want to change?

Now that you've taken responsibility for where you've found your-self in life, and figured out how much you want to change, it's important to figure out exactly *why* you want to change and what specifically about your career or life you want to reduce or replace.

If you go back to the number you figured out during the exercise in Chapter 2, it's now time to break that down further into the specific reasons behind your desire to change, because it's only by looking at the root causes of your problems that you'll be able to find a solution that fixes them rather than just papering over the cracks.

In my experience working with thousands of companies over the past 15 years, firstly as a lawyer and in recent times as a business advisor, one of the most common problems I see is that we have a tendency as a society to treat symptoms rather than root causes.

If you go to see the doctor with a sore knee, the chances are he or she will prescribe pain killers to deal with the pain without identifying the cause of the problem.

So, we're going to get right to the root rather than messing around with drugs that only serve to numb the discomfort.

It's also crucial that you consider how much you want to change. It makes a difference whether you were a zero or a six in the earlier exercise (or a higher number if you decided to take the plunge and read the book anyway). If you're a zero it may be that radical changes are necessary because you are fundamentally in the wrong place for you to thrive, whereas if you were a six because I wouldn't let you have a seven, it may be that only small tweaks to your current role are needed to maximise your happiness and fulfilment.

Which means that it's exercise time again. Don't worry, I don't mean I'm going to get you to do burpees or squat on the spot, we'll save that for the live event. All you need for the moment is a pen and a piece of paper, your phone or some other device on which you can write. I'll allow a computer or a tablet, but you get bonus marks if you do it on a typewriter. I've got no idea why, I just like the thought of you doing this on a typewriter as though it's 1974.

Exercise

Anyway, on the assumption that you're not going to do it on a typewriter, here's a little chart for you to write in or which you can copy out if you'd like more space. You'll need the information you come up with here to use later on, so I'd recommend either copying it onto your computer or writing it on a large piece of paper. If you'd like a lovely version that's ready to print for you to use, go to *www.changeyourcareer.org/essence*.

Current Number ____	The 7 Secrets to Change Your Career *www.changeyourcareer.org/essence*		Target Number ____
Everything you dislike, hate or despise about your current job and/or life:	(We'll fill this column later)	(We'll fill this column later)	(We'll fill this column later)
1.			
2.			
3.			
4.			
5.			

Current Number _____	The 7 Secrets to Change Your Career *www.changeyourcareer.org/essence*		Target Number _____
Everything you dislike, hate or despise about your current job and/or life:	(We'll fill this column later)	(We'll fill this column later)	(We'll fill this column later)
6.			
7.			
8.			
9.			
10.			

Write your current number from the exercise in Chapter 2 in the top left corner, and the number you want to reach once you've transformed your life in the top right. As a hint, the number in the top right should be a nine or a 10 depending on whether you're aiming for the most-dreamiest of dream lives or something a step below that.

I'll accept an eight if you're coming from four or below, but only if you'll be satisfied with an eight after going through all of the changes over the coming chapters. (Please bear in mind, though, that if you do decide to go for an eight or nine at this point, my aim by the end of the book will be to convince you that a 10 is the correct target anyway. We might as well aim for the stars and only settle for the moon if we need to.)

Now, in the first column, take five minutes to write down everything that you dislike, hate or despise about your current job and/ or life, depending on how deep into the rabbit hole you want to go. I'd recommend timing it on your phone or other clock-type device, and doing this in a quiet place with no distractions. The important thing, again, is not to think about it too much and just go with whatever pops into your head. Remember that there are no wrong answers, and this exercise is for you and no one else, so it's essential and absolutely imperative that you are completely honest with yourself.

Now, this is a tricky conversation for us to have before you even start the exercise.

The problem I've found with being honest with yourself is that, if you're anything like me, you are probably pretty fucked up at this stage in your life, maybe without even knowing it. If you've bought this book and are eagerly working through it ready for your life to be transformed, there is a very good chance that you don't have a clue what you actually want or truly know what being true to yourself is (as opposed to doing things for everyone else), even if you're doing that subconsciously.

I say this because about 10 weeks before I started to write this book I began seeing a psychotherapist.

Now, your reaction to that sentence is likely to partly depend on where you're from. If you're British, like me, and especially if you're a British male, there's a very good chance that you recoiled in your seat, immediately wanted to scratch your own eyes out and were tempted to throw the book out of the nearest window in case you caught whatever it is I got that made me soft.

I know, I know. If you'd have asked me three months ago whether I'd ever go to see a therapist I'd have told you that I'm not a soft American who wants to sit on a couch telling some stranger about his private life (sorry if you're an American, but that's one of the stereotypes that some other countries have of you – I never said it was fair or accurate). But it's only been since sitting in that therapist's office that I've been able to figure out exactly how messed up I'd become and how much of my life and how many of the decisions I'd made over the past 30 years hadn't been of my own free will.

It has blown my mind.

Now this is probably beyond the scope of this book, but I don't really care. My job is to help you to transform your career and your life, so I'll just say things and you can pick and choose which bits are for you and which bits aren't. For those of you who might be open to the idea of really getting stuck in to getting to the root causes of your problems, I can't recommend highly enough going to see someone who doesn't know you at all but who has all of the requisite skills and experience to guide you through the psychological minefield of your past. Without doing that you might never get to a nine or 10 on the happiness or fulfilment scale, but it's beyond my current pay grade to be able to advise either way on that.

For my part, I always envisaged going to see a "shrink" as a really negative thing that would creep me out and wouldn't do me any good, but the therapist I've been seeing every week as part of my new healthy lifestyle routine is a really normal bloke with a similar background to me. I quickly built a great rapport with him, so I can sit and chat about anything I want without fear of being judged or anything I say being repeated to someone I don't want it to be repeated to. He can challenge and guide me in ways my friends and family just don't have the expertise or experience to do, which is invaluable.

If you stop and think for a second how many things go through your mind every day or every week that you never say to anyone, I bet it's loads. We tell ourselves that these things are just little bits and pieces, just tiny problems or miniscule complaints that everyone has, but the problem is that they all add up. Slowly over time the little things become the big things without us even realising it. Especially when they've been building up for decades.

Through the work I've been doing recently I've realised that I've lived most of my life trying to please my parents and my wider family, mainly to my complete detriment. Loads of decisions, from deciding to be a lawyer (although that decision was made before I can even remember), to getting married when I was stressed out of my mind and shouldn't have been organising a night at the races let alone taking on the pressure of a flash wedding for 90 people in Spain, all the way through to tiny decisions every week to do things or not to do things in case it upset the people I love.

So, this is my way of saying that when you write down anything in this exercise or in exercises in the following chapters, go with your gut and not with your head. Your gut is more likely to be in contact with the little person inside you who's still trying desperately to get out and tell the real truth, whereas your head is likely to be run largely by your ego which intellectualises everything and convinces you to do things that really aren't good for you.

You'll see that there's space for 10 things in the table above, but don't let that affect what you write. There are no right or wrong answers, so if you've got more than 10 things make sure you get them all down, and if you've got fewer than 10 that's fine, too. If you're stuck for things to write, start with the moment you wake up in the morning and walk yourself in your mind through your day, focusing at each step on the feeling in your stomach when you think of each one.

Every time you hit something that makes your gut churn or makes you feel angry, sad or depressed, write it down. For me, it would have started straight away with *"having to get up before I've had enough sleep"*, followed immediately by *"checking emails as soon as I roll out of bed which immediately start to piss me off"*. Write everything down from the smallest annoyances to the biggest problems that make you angry (your dick head boss, your commute to work, your stupid colleagues, your kids watching you on the toilet). You can be as mean as you like at this stage because no one else is going to see this and, if nothing else, it will be therapeutic to get it all out of your system.

Once you've got going you might find you need more than one piece of paper.

Ready? Get started and come back when you're done.

* * *

Have you finished?

Really? Now don't be one of those people who read something like this and just skip past the exercises because you think you'll do it later or some other bullshit excuse. I used to do that then realised I wasn't getting anything out of the books that wanted to take me through a process, which is what will happen to you if you don't go through this a step at a time. If you skip ahead without doing each exercise in turn you won't get the same impact or value, because your brain will be thinking too much about the next bit before focusing on the current task, which isn't ideal.

I know that your ego now might be telling you that this bit is just for the other people and not for you, or that you're so clever that you can do it all at once and it'll all be fine. That used to be me as well, but I promise just telling your ego to shut up for 10 minutes will do you the world of good. I've now got mine down to having about an hour a day in supervised play time, which makes him much more manageable and also makes him play nicer with his friends while the rest of me can get on with living a happy life without him driving us everywhere and driving everyone else mad.

If you didn't do the exercise go back and do it now, then we'll move on.

* * *

All done? If you haven't done it I'm going to get the person I've sent to watch you to report back, so make sure it is done.

Right, so you've got your list of the things you don't like about what you currently do. Now to dig deeper into each one.

In the next column take as much time as you need to write down what specifically you don't like about each point that you noted. Using my examples above, I'd write next to *"having to get up before I've had enough sleep"* the further specific detail of *"I don't like getting up early and prefer to stay in bed longer without having to be in work for a certain time"*.

If you hate your boss, write down specifically what it is that you hate about them. Again, go into as much detail as possible and use more space if you need to.

Ready? Go.

Current Number ____	The 7 Secrets to Change Your Career *www.changeyourcareer.org/essence*		Target Number ____
Everything you dislike, hate or despise about your current job and/or life:	What specifically is it that you don't like about it:	(We'll fill this column later)	(We'll fill this column later)
1.			
2.			

Current Number ____	The 7 Secrets to Change Your Career www.changeyourcareer.org/essence		Target Number ____
Everything you dislike, hate or despise about your current job and/or life:	What specifically is it that you don't like about it:	(We'll fill this column later)	(We'll fill this column later)
3.			
4.			
5.			
6.			
7.			

Current Number ____	The 7 Secrets to Change Your Career *www.changeyourcareer.org/essence*		Target Number ____
Everything you dislike, hate or despise about your current job and/or life:	What specifically is it that you don't like about it:	(We'll fill this column later)	(We'll fill this column later)
8.			
9.			
10.			

All done? Great.

How are you feeling? Has it helped to just get down on paper exactly what it is you don't like about what you currently do every day? I find with most people that going through this exercise properly is half of the battle, because while we can be miserable in our lives on a daily basis, we very rarely actually sit down to identify what it is specifically that we don't like that's weighing us down, and it's only by identifying the root causes that we can hope to solve the problems and move on.

Our problems tend to feel like massive dark clouds floating above our heads every day as a constant grey menace. But once we start reaching up and pulling on the threads hanging down in order to put them into some sort of order, we notice that we start to create gaps in the storm clouds that begin to let the bright sunlight peek through.

Which takes us to the next part of the exercise, which I call *"Is that really the reason or are you kidding yourself?"*. I really wanted to get a swear word into that sentence as I wrote it but it didn't seem to fit. Never mind, I'll add one in later.

So, this is the really tricky bit, and ties in to my earlier chat about seeing a therapist. You see, I've discovered very recently that loads of the things that I thought were doing my head in (I'll have to ask my editor if that phrase translates to other countries, but I think you'll get the gist of it) weren't actually doing my head in at all. To use an example from my home life, I've complained for years that my wife is too untidy, that there's always a mess everywhere and the house isn't tidy enough for me. But I've discovered lately that was a big pile of bollocks (I think that phrase definitely translates).

It turns out that I'm not actually that tidy after all. What was happening was down to carrying around shit from my childhood about keeping things tidy. Because I'm probably a six out of 10 on the tidiness scale (with 10 being super-duper OCD tidy and zero being living in a dump) and my wife is a 5.9, I could always just point at her and say *"you're really messy"* (I've made myself sound nicer there than I was in practice), when the reality was that it was never that big a deal.

The reason I made it a big deal was other shit I had to sort out that was coming out through frustrations like tidiness. The root cause of *"you're really messy"* turned out to be *"I don't feel like I'm worthy of love"* which, obviously, is a bit of a mind-fuck in itself.

It's tough because without digging deep into your psyche and figuring out everything that makes you tick, it may be that you won't find out until some future point that something you thought you hated you didn't really, but that's okay.

The purpose of this entire exercise is to help to get you to a place where you're no longer afraid to make changes (you will absolutely love Secret 4 which is all about that point). When in the future something comes up that makes you think *"oh shit, it wasn't Steve that was the problem after all, it was me"* you'll be well equipped to put it down to experience and tweak something else without it being such a big deal, all the time edging towards that dream target number 10.

Always remember that very few things in life are irreparable as long as when you change things you do it in a kind and generous way. If you don't actually run out of work screaming *"you're all a bunch of fuck-faced arseholes and I never want to see you again!"*, then you'll pretty much be fine and can always go back to what you were doing before if needs be.

So, here's the last part of the current exercise. In the third column, next to each point ask yourself the question *"why?"* five times to get to the actual root cause. The root might come up for some of the points before you've got to the fifth *"why?"*, which is fine.

This might take a bit of thinking outside the box, so remember again that there are no right or wrong answers. For example, for my waking up early point, if I started with *"I don't like getting up early"* and asked why, it would have gone like this:

Why? Because I like to go to bed late

Why? Because my life is stressful, I work long hours and by the time I get home I want to watch some TV to relax

Why? Because otherwise I think my life is a complete waste of time

Why? Because I hate my job

Why? Because it wasn't something I wanted to do in the first place

If you keep asking why for long enough you will eventually get to *"because life is essentially a pointless exercise and we don't know why we're here or why we're doing any of this"*, so I'd recommend stopping once you get to what feels like the root cause in the general scheme of things, otherwise we'll end up in an existential crisis together instead of creating more time to play catch in the garden and paint pictures of daffodils.

In my example, it becomes apparent fairly quickly that not wanting to get up early is driven generally by the fact that I hate my overall job, so that might not actually be a key factor for a future, happy life (which is the point of the exercise). It turns out that I actually don't mind getting up early if it's for something I love, although ideally getting out of bed before 8am isn't really for me.

Take as long as you need for this. I've set out below a few examples to help you. Depending on what the specific thing is that you don't like, you might have to expand the *"why"* question to *"why do you dislike/hate that?"* or *"why does that annoy you?"* in order for the exercise to work effectively, as shown in example 3 below.

Example 1

What you dislike, hate or despise about your current job and/ or life:

I hate having to get up before I've had enough sleep.

What specifically is it that you don't like about it:

I don't like getting up early.

Why, why, why, why, why?

Why? Because I like to go to bed late.

Why? Because my life is stressful, I work long hours and by the time I get home I want to watch some TV to relax.

Why? Because otherwise I think my life is a complete waste of time.

Why? Because I hate my job.

Why? Because it wasn't something I wanted to do in the first place.

Example 2

What you dislike, hate or despise about your current job and/ or life:

I hate travelling so far to get to work.

What specifically is it that you don't like about it:

I feel like it wastes my time.

Why, why, why, why, why?

Why? Because there are other things I'd rather be doing.

Why? Because there are things in life I want to do that I don't have time to do.

Why? Because I don't have enough time outside of work to do the things I want.

Why? Because I waste loads of time watching TV and playing on my phone.

Why? Because by the time I get home from work I'm tired and fed up, so don't want to do anything else.

Example 3

What you dislike, hate or despise about your current job and/ or life:

No matter how hard I work I always get paid the same.

What specifically is it that you don't like about it:

I feel like I'm not paid what I'm worth.

Why, why, why, why, why?

Why? Because the firm charges clients £200 an hour for my time and I'm only paid a fraction of that.

Why do you dislike that? Because I feel like I'm worth more than the fraction I get paid.

Why? Because I've worked hard all of my life to get where I am.

Why does that annoy you? Because I thought after all these years of work I'd be further ahead than I am right now.

All done? What you should hopefully have ended up with is a comprehensive list of everything that you dislike about your current job and/or life (depending on how far you wanted to take the exercise) as well as the root cause of each problem. If you got stuck on anything, remember you can get in touch using my email address at the end of the book.

You will no doubt also think of more things as the days pass, which you should add to the list as and when they come to you, going through the same process each time. Keep the thought in your mind as you're going about your daily life and just start to notice the little things that wind you up, aggravate or annoy you. It might be little things that you'd forgotten about, like sharing a toaster every morning which means your toast always gets burnt, or never getting a seat on the train or bus on the way to work. Whatever it is, capture it and go through the process to get to the root cause of each one.

It's also really important at this stage to take a few minutes to reflect on what you've just done and to give yourself credit for it. It's never easy to inspect your own life and to identify all of the things that you think are wrong with it. It takes courage and a strong heart to be able to do that, and I think it's imperative that whenever we do anything good we should make a note of it and allow ourselves to be pleased with what we've done.

Over the years I know that I've been terrible at giving myself credit for anything positive I've ever achieved. If you're anything like me, you'll no doubt find yourself thinking that anything you can do is just standard, just a normal thing that anyone can do. But the reality is that's simply not true.

Most people in life aren't analysing their own challenges and problems and working on ways to fix them. Most people throughout the ages have just grumbled every day about the same old things over and over again, until they retire and eventually die, no doubt grumbling about how the inside of their coffin isn't as bright as they thought it would be, and how heaven is a lot colder than they imagined.

I'm as guilty of this as everyone else, which is why I like to remind us all to take stock of the good things we're doing instead of just focusing on the things that have gone wrong. The truth is that you'll notice the bad things anyway, so it's important to celebrate the little wins, and going through an in-depth analysis of your career and/or life to pull out all of the grimy bits is certainly more than a little win, so make sure you congratulate yourself for a job well done.

It's okay to be proud of yourself for achieving something, however big or small.

Now, put your work somewhere safe to come back to later on for the exciting, hopeful part of the journey. Before then, though, we need to do some counting …

5

SECRET 3
COUNT THE NUMBERS

Ah, numbers.

Your attitude towards this chapter will probably depend on how much you liked maths in school.

If you aren't troubled by counting you will no doubt dance through the next few pages like a pixie in a field but, if that isn't you, look at the next few minutes as a necessary evil in the grand plan to change your life and I promise it will be far less painful than you might think. I will keep it as short as humanly possible.

The point of this chapter is very simple.

Generally speaking, when I see people looking to make great changes in their lives, careers or businesses, they don't spend enough time on the detail. It's like when I'm chatting to entrepreneurs who think that becoming the next Steve Jobs is all about blue sky thinking, dreaming big and ignoring everything else. Without the dreams you can't achieve anything significant, but the problem is that the dreams in themselves aren't enough without the substance behind them. It's not all about putting pool tables in your office to become the next Apple.

It's a bit like if you want to win a gold medal at the Olympics. Without the blue sky goal of wanting to win the medal you'll never start the process but, once you've decided on that goal, the reality of achieving it means getting up every day at 5am through the wind, rain and snow, on dark mornings when no one is watching and nobody cares, for four solid years, all for the sake of a few minutes in front of the eyes of the world to have a crack at the big objective.

There'll be plenty of time later for drifting away in your mind to far foreign lands in search of your dream life. For now, though, we need to plot out how you're going to take the first steps towards getting there, which means numbers. We need to figure out together what is the minimum amount you need to survive each month to implant in your mind a specific figure to work towards instead of a make-believe number that might otherwise be stuck in your head.

One thing that holds lots of people back from making changes in their lives is a myth about how much they need to survive. If you are currently paid as an employee, I bet that when you discuss your pay or even think about it during times of contemplation, you talk about the big, pretty number that your employer says it pays you, which makes you feel all lovely and warm.

Am I right?

So, whether that's £20,000, £50,000 or £100,000, it's not really relevant. And it's not relevant what the big number is if you currently work for yourself either.

Exercise

The most important number to start with is the number that ends up in your bank account each month after all of your taxes and other deductions have been paid.

If you're an employee that should basically mean the sum paid into your bank by your employer, provided that you're in a country where employee taxes are deducted at source before the balance is paid to you.

If you're not in a country like that, or if you're self-employed and take your own money out of a company, it's imperative that you calculate how much you are earning each month after making an allowance for all of the taxes and other deductions you need to make.

This is really important so make sure it's right, because we'll be building everything else around it in the following chapters.

If you're not sure what that number is, speak to your accountant or have a look online at how you should be calculating it in your country. If you're still not sure after all of that, send me an email to the address at the end of the book.

Once you've got that number, make a note of it using the table on the next page or something like it. If you want to print or download a version, go to *www.changeyourcareer.org/count*.

Current income: _____		
Cost of going to work:		
Net disposable income:		
Essential outgoings (non-negotiable):		
		Required income:_____
Essential outgoings (negotiable):		
		Required income:_____

The Dad Count

Next is something I learnt very recently from my very own dad.

Mr Cope senior retired a few years ago having completely nailed the traditional way of living your life. He worked hard for a limited number of employers over his working career, accumulating as many pensions as he could along the way.

I definitely did not take after him when it came to career or pension planning.

I was chatting to him a few weeks ago about how things were going and he commented in passing that he's better off financially now than he ever was when he was working.

"How is that possible?" I asked

"Well, the pensions I've got have replaced most of my income, but now I don't have to pay to get to work every day, buy lunch when I'm there or contribute to everyone's birthday and leaving collections."

I'd never thought of any of those things. Have you?

When we talk about our income from a job, we tend to just talk about the gross salary. Not only is that misleading, as set out above, but it also doesn't take into account the cost of travelling to and from work, which comes out of our taxed, net income.

By that, I mean that when you pay for your transport to work you're using the money you've been paid by work after the taxman has taken his cut (assuming for this part that you are currently a paid employee). The same applies to the lunches you buy and the contributions you make to buying cakes for the office.

It all adds up, so you should tot it up and deduct it from the amount that's paid into your bank account each month. That way, you can see exactly how much you get to spend from your salary. If you don't know exactly how much you spend on lunch or on buying cakes for the office, use your best estimate.

You might wonder at this stage what the point of this part of the exercise is because, no matter what you do, you'll still need to buy lunch and travel to work. The reality is that that's not necessarily the case, so by understanding all of these numbers you can factor them into what you decide to do next.

For example, if you decide to work from home every day in the future, you save all transport costs, no longer have to chip into anyone's leaving collection and can make your own lunch at home. Depending on the tax regime in your country, there are also often tax benefits of running your own company versus being paid a salary by an employer, in particular in relation to expenses that you can pay direct from the company rather than through your taxed income.

Next, you're going to need your last two or three months' bank statements, so you'll need to download them or print them off before going on. If your monthly income and outgoings are pretty standard, you might be able to get away with using the last full month or two, but using three full months helps to make sure that there's nothing you're forgetting about that might be important.

Done that?

Great.

The next step is to go through whatever months you've decided to go through and separate your outgoings into three categories: Essential (non-negotiable), Essential (negotiable) and Non-Essential.

I'd define each category as follows:

Essential (non-negotiable) – things like your mortgage payments or rent, utility bills like gas, electricity and water, credit card and loan repayments and anything essential to your daily life that cannot be compromised, including subscriptions that can't be cancelled easily.

Essential (negotiable) – things like food costs, clothing spend, subscriptions that you might be able to cancel (such as gym membership or Netflix). Basically, anything that you spend at the moment on things that you might usually consider essential, but could cut back on given the right motivation.

Non-essential – everything else like socialising, eating out, gambling etc. Basically, things which you are pissing your money away on but if I put a gun to your head and told you to save some money you could stop immediately.

*   *   *

Depending on how hardcore you want to approach this there might well be things that can move between the categories later, but we can address that once you've been through the initial exercise.

Take your time now to go through the statements and fill out the table. It's important that you do this accurately so don't rush. This is also where going through two or three months' worth of statements will help to make sure you don't miss anything, because you can compare one month against another for accuracy.

*   *   *

Once you've done that and completed the table, add up what your total Essential (non-negotiable) outgoings are and what your Essential (negotiable) outgoings are and insert them in the relevant section.

These will be your guide numbers for when we get to Chapter 7. The first is basically what you need as a minimum income to survive. The second is an additional amount that you might need but could be negotiable. The way I'd look at it is that if you can earn enough when changing careers to still pay for Netflix, that's great, but if you need to sacrifice it for a few months for the sake of transforming from a miserable life to a much happier and fulfilling one, then it's a price worth paying. If at this point you're thinking to yourself *"but I can't live without Netflix!"* then it might be that you need to reconsider how much you want to change from the life you're currently living.

But that's more for the next secret ...

6

SECRET 4
RATIONALISATION & EXCUSES

Why haven't you changed yet?

This is my first book so I'm not sure if naming a chapter as my favourite is the same as picking a favourite child, but I haven't got any kids yet and I can't believe people who say they don't have a favourite one, so I'm just going to go ahead and say that this is my favourite. Not that it's the most fun or the most exciting, but it is the most important. For me, this is the section that is the difference between the people who take action to make changes in their lives and those who just talk about it.

I went to see a world-renowned speaker and entrepreneur a few weeks ago who I absolutely love, Gary Vaynerchuk (or Gary Vee to his ardent fans), and he repeated something that I've heard him say many times before, that 99 per cent of the people who listen to him every day and are pumped up by what he says never do anything about it.

They listen to it all, they get motivated, then they … do nothing.

It tied into something I'd been working on for a while and some things that have become clear to me in recent months about different parts of my life, which all come together in this chapter.

What are the reasons for most people never changing? If there are millions of people watching the likes of Gary Vee every day, following Tim Ferriss and being inspired by Tony Robbins, why are so many of them not moving forward to change their lives? What is it that's holding people back?

Most importantly to me right now, what has been holding you back? And why haven't you changed before? In what ways are you rationalising the misery you're keeping yourself in and making excuses for not taking the steps needed to change?

Let's jump straight into the deep end.

Addiction, Family, Fear, Ego, Insecurity and the Sunk Cost Fallacy

My favourite parts of my favourite child. Let's start in reverse order.

Part 1 – The Sunk Cost Fallacy

It's September 2015. I've just completed the sale of my law firm to a larger firm in the city. I'm pretty happy with the deal I negotiated given how absolutely terrible I've been feeling for so long.

They've already got offices so don't need mine, and the landlord has told me that it doesn't want to keep the fancy fit-out I'd installed just a few years earlier so it's time for the glass walls and plaster board partitions to come down. I've managed to sell the expensive glass for a knock down price to a company down the corridor; another lesson in things not to spend money on when starting a business.

So, all that's left are the walls that created the board room and the smaller meeting room away from the main area where I and the rest of the team sat.

I'm standing there on a cold Saturday morning, all alone in the office I'd built, taking in my surroundings. As I walk in there's a glass plaque just outside the main, dark wooden door that shows the logo of the firm in dark purple and white. I'd picked purple after researching colours and finding that it elicited a feeling of trust in customers. I knew that blue did the same but loads of other firms used blue and the whole point was to be different.

As I step through the door the office wraps around me in the shape of a letter 'L', with one length going off to my left and the other behind me to the right.

Before moving the team into the office a few years earlier I fitted a kitchen on the far-left wall so that we didn't need to use the shared facilities down the corridor. It's just a few high gloss white units with a sink, fridge and microwave, but it looks good.

The kitchen is separated from the open plan work space for the rest of the team by a plaster board wall, painted white to match the rest of the office with a small doorway as the entrance.

To the right-hand corner, opposite where I stood, is where my office used to be, separated from the rest by a glass wall with that frosting you see in offices everywhere.

I think back now and wonder whether it was the right thing to do to physically separate myself from the rest of the team. There are mixed views on it depending on who you listen to, but I don't think it mattered in the grand scheme of things.

In the last section of the 'L' shape behind me to my right are the board room and a smaller, second meeting room, sectioned off from the rest of the office by another glass wall and a few plaster board walls to maintain the confidentiality of clients who came in for meetings and to make sure that sound didn't travel between rooms. It's definitely not a good idea in the legal profession to have confidential conversations overheard by people next door.

As I stand there looking at the remaining plasterboard walls, the glass having already been removed, I have a flashback to where it all started, sitting in the spare bedroom of my city centre flat with that blank piece of paper. It was all so exciting and promising then. I thought I was going to take over the world.

Yet here I am, the master of my own domain to which I've come today to rip down with my own hands.

I'm standing in an old pair of white trainers, blue jeans and a white t-shirt I used to wear for painting when I was doing property developments a couple of years before. In my left hand is a portable speaker ready for my iPhone to be plugged into and in my right is a claw hammer; my tool of choice for tearing down the physical walls I'd built and which had come to represent the mental and emotional barricades that had been towering over me for so long.

Today is the day I'm breaking free.

I decided having had my awakening and realising that if I built my own prison I could also demolish it, that it would be symbolic and therapeutic to take some time on my own to smash into those walls until there were none left.

I plug the speaker into a socket in the corner of the room, put on my high energy motivational music that had been used for so long just to drag me out of bed each morning, and I get to work.

As I pull my protective goggles over my eyes and survey the main board room wall in front of me, painted purple to match the logo of the company, I can feel all of those years of anger, resentment and misery in the pit of my stomach. I can feel the tension across my shoulders and the intense pain stabbing through my right shoulder, throbbing as it always has.

I take a deep breath as *Eye Of The Tiger* begins playing on my play-list, gripping the hammer tightly in my right hand to make sure that it doesn't slip at the wrong moment, and with every ounce of frustration and fury firing through my veins I raise it above my head and thunder it down onto the wall, crashing through the plaster board and shattering the illusion of perfection that the previously smooth wall represents in my mind.

It feels incredible.

As the tension starts to escape through every pore of my body I keep crashing the hammer into the wall, one, two, three times. My heart is racing, there's dust everywhere and I'm screaming the lyrics of the song at the top of my voice.

I fucking hate the world. The stupid fucking world and it's stupid fucking rules. That's what trapped me in this place for so long; feeling like I had to please my family, doing things I hated every single day of my life just to make other people proud and to feed my ego that had been spiralling out of control over decades.

Well, no more. From now on I'm going to do what I want to do. I grip the exposed plasterboard and start ripping the walls down with my bare hands, piece after piece, section after section. I feel like I'm ripping down all of the limitations in my mind that have tortured me silently for so long.

It feels amazing.

The plaster boards come down bit by bit and expose the metal frames that they're built on. When the contractors put them in they told me it was worth paying extra for the metal because they can be taken out and used again if you need to relocate in the future. That story obviously changed by the time I wanted to take them out though. Not worth the hassle then. Too much labour cost.

The thought of it feeds me with even more anger and energy to strike one blow after the next into the frame, making the ceiling shake. I'd usually care whether I was disturbing anyone else. I'd usually be insecure about what others thought of me. But not today. Today I am on a mission to demolish every part of this prison so that it can't hurt me or anyone else ever again.

I'm there for hours. Smashing things to bits and making a complete mess. Swinging the hammer over my head time and time again, before ripping at the plaster board with my hands. It's like therapy. It's so good that I consider starting a business where people can just turn up at a city centre location and smash things with a hammer to relieve stress.

As the evening draws in, I sit in the corner of the room with my back against the wall, with my protective goggles resting on the top of my head and my elbows resting on my knees, surveying the destruction in front of me. A smile creeps across my face.

Piles of plaster board, bits of metal and a layer of dust covering everything, but no more walls.

It feels good. So good. It feels like I'm actually breaking out of that place once and for all. At long last taking down the barriers of the life I never wanted so that I can build my own from scratch.

*   *   *

Does any of this resonate with you? Do you ever feel like ripping everything down so that you can start again? Of standing in the middle of the road and screaming at the top of your voice with all of the power your lungs can muster?

*   *   *

A few days later, after my dad and wife had helped to clear up the mess, putting it all in heavy duty rubble sacks and dumping them in a skip in the car park to the rear of the building, I'm back in the office which is now just an empty 'L' shape just as it was when I first viewed it, apart from the gloss white kitchen which is still there at the landlord's request.

All that's left to do is for the stacks of boxes of client files that are sitting in the far left corner, away from the previous days' destruction, to be taken away by an archive company.

I'm waiting inside the office when someone knocks on the door.

I open it to see a man in what I'd say is his late fifties or early sixties, about five foot eight inches tall with a good head of white and grey hair. He's what I'd imagine Elvis's little brother might look like in his retirement years. He's wearing a light grey uniform that's darker than his hair and matches the grey autumn sky outside, and he flashes me a warm smile as he introduces himself as being from the archive company. We start chatting and he tells me all about the business his son has built and how he helps out sometimes for something to do to get him out from underneath his wife's feet.

He asks what I did and why I'm moving out, and I give him the one-minute summary version about growing tired of the legal profession and setting up an online business.

"So, you're just quitting it altogether?" he says.

"Well, I'll be doing some consultancy work for the buyer as part of the sale to make sure that clients are handed across properly but, other than that, yep, I'm leaving it all behind."

"But didn't it take years of study to get where you are? I've heard it takes six years just to qualify, then you've built your own business and you're just throwing it all away?"

"Erm, yep, basically."

He stares at me with a look that's a cross between pity and annoyance. I know it because I've already seen it on the faces of my parents and other members of my family when I first told them about my plans.

"What an absolute waste that is."

*   *   *

And that's it. That's the sunk cost fallacy in one real life anecdote.

It's the idea that because you've spent a certain amount of time or money doing something, you now must continue to do that same thing until some future point in time which is usually either not defined at all or not defined well enough and, unless or until you reach that moment, you cannot quit what you're doing regardless of how miserable that thing is making you, how much money you're losing or how poor your health has become.

It's one of the most bananas theories known to man and is usually held, in my experience, by an older generation that was programmed to work for one company its whole life before retiring with a pension and a gold-plated clock to say thanks for 50 years of service.

It is also one of the most dangerous concepts in the world, and is responsible for a huge number of people doing things they hate, whether that's continuing in a job that they should have left years ago, or sticking in a relationship that died before the invention of Netflix. (Come to think of it, maybe Netflix's USP was actually keeping unhappy couples together through the medium of box set addictions. There could be a book in that.)

Anyway, the point of this is that it is completely illogical for us to make decisions going forward based on decisions we have made in the past. In the most basic example, if you are playing roulette in a casino and you've lost £50, the sunk cost fallacy says that you need to keep playing roulette until you've won that £50 back.

If you've ever played roulette, you'll know that's not a very wise idea and is likely to lead to you losing your house.

If you've lost £50 playing roulette and you want to win it back, the best thing you can do is to take a step back, assess the situation and ask yourself whether continuing to play the game that has so far cost you so much is the best way back, or whether there might be another, easier, more reliable way to make £50.

The answer is almost always, yes – there is a much better way. You don't need to make lost money back using the same method by which you lost it in the first place, and only a trick of the mind makes you think that playing a losing game time and time again is a good idea.

Does this make sense to you? Have you ever found your brain convincing you that you should carry on doing something that your gut knows is wrong, but you decide to anyway because the brain should really know what it's talking about bearing in mind it's meant to have all of the smart bits and everything?

Don't listen to your brain and, even more importantly, do not listen to other people's brains.

Other people's brains are one of the biggest enemies you'll face in your battle to break free of a miserable career and life and bounce, joyously, into a happier life. This is because most people are living miserable lives, and their brains don't want you making them look like idiots, so will do everything they can to convince your brain that you don't know what you're doing.

Don't listen.

To paraphrase Nancy Reagan, JUST SAY NO TO BRAINS.

We'll talk more about brains and their dangers in the next part.

For the purposes of the sunk cost fallacy, though, it's important to identify whether you are, or have been, holding back from making a decision about the present or the future because of time and/or money that you've invested in the past.

Have you done that?

A classic example in my first career was the idea that you've been doing this job for so long that you can't stop until you've been made partner. Now, don't get me wrong, I know plenty of people who actually enjoy being a lawyer (I think they might actually be insane though) and becoming a partner was always part of their goal.

But they're not the people I'm talking about. If you're happy in what you do and you have a goal to aim for, that's a good thing. It's effectively where all of this will lead.

The sunk cost fallacy applies if you're doing something that you hate, or even something you dislike, and you feel as though you can't move away from doing that thing because of all of the time and money you've already invested in it.

It's an absolute load of bollocks and I'll tell you why.

When I decided to quit being a lawyer, they didn't send an army of people to my house in the middle of the night with huge spot lights and surgical equipment to remove from my mind all of the stuff I'd learned in the previous 15 years. The *Men in Black* didn't hijack me in a dark alley and zap my brain with one of their laser pens to wipe my memory.

When you stop doing the thing that makes you miserable, you still get to take all of the good stuff with you to the next thing. All of the experiences you've had, good and bad, all of the lessons you've learned and all of the knowledge you've gained carries forward to be used on whatever you do next, which will hopefully utilise your skills and knowledge without making you absolutely miserable.

To use myself as an example, the work I do now uses loads of the skills and experiences I gained throughout my legal career. I learned how to deal with clients, how to negotiate and how to speak in front of an audience under pressure, to name but a few. In fact, when I was choosing what to do next in my life after reflecting on my past experiences, as well as identifying the parts of my old life that I hated I also looked at the parts that I enjoyed. I always enjoyed solving problems and meeting with clients to find creative solutions to things, but I hated reading long cases and having to review and draft documents. Which meant that I just needed to design something that avoided me doing the heavily lawyer-y bit and focussed on me doing the 'helping people in meetings' bit.

We'll delve into all of that more in the next chapter as well.

So, when you catch yourself thinking, or hear anyone else saying, that it would be a waste to change from what you do now because of all of the time or money you've already invested in it, just think of all of the skills you've picked up that wouldn't be wasted at all and, in fact, you could use to catapult yourself into your new life rather than wasting anymore time or energy doing something you hate.

Does that all make sense?

Good.

Time to talk about those pesky brains …

Part 2 – Ego and Insecurity

Ooh, this is a fun one. Let's start with a question.

Do you consider yourself to be egotistical or arrogant?

If the answer is yes, congratulations on being honest and self-aware, you probably don't need most of this next section but it'll be worth reading for entertainment purposes.

If you answered 'no', prepare to find out things about yourself that you're not going to like very much. I hope by this point you trust me enough to know that what I'm about to say I do so with love and with the sole intention of helping you to move forward. I'm that mate who's happy to tell you the truth that you need to hear even though it's uncomfortable for everyone which, ironically, I tend not to be in real life because I don't like the awkwardness. Luckily for you I'm not in the room with you when you read this, though, so I'm safe to crack on.

This is about excuses and something that occurred to me recently when listening to people making excuses for the things they're not willing to do to change their lives for the better. It had never occurred to me before but since the penny dropped I'm seeing it everywhere.

Just take a second to think about the last time you made an excuse for not doing something. It could be anything, but the ones I tend to see relate to reasons people give for not changing something in their business that would help them, not doing something differently in their personal life that could solve many of their problems or, a very common one, not doing as much exercise or eating as healthily as someone else.

Do you have any of your own you can think of?

What I've noticed is that lots of excuses start with a reference to the excuse-maker's circumstances and why their circumstances are far worse than everybody else's, which justifies whatever it is they're using as an excuse.

They go something like this:

"I know Flo does five hours of exercise a week, but I've got a really busy job so don't have the time."

"It's fine for Jimmy to say he changed how he bills his customers, but my business is more complicated than that so it can't be done."

"You might be able to take time to start a business, but I've got a four year-old to look after so there's no chance."

And, my personal favourite:

"Well, you're just lucky because …"

Sound familiar?

What occurred to me about every excuse like these is that they're all egotistical. They all imply that the person making the excuse is far more important, far busier or works far harder than everyone else, which justifies whatever it is they don't want to do.

Ego, with a touch of arrogance.

Has it stung yet? No? Not Enough? Okay, I'll carry on.

When you tell yourself something to justify why you can't do what someone else is doing, what you're actually doing is telling yourself that your circumstances are so special that they elevate you above everyone else. It is a camouflaged sense of self-importance that you're almost certainly not acknowledging as such.

It's saying, without expressly saying out loud, *"Yes, I know that they do it, but if they were as busy/stressed/important as me they wouldn't be able to".*

How fucking arrogant.

Whenever you look at someone else doing something that you aren't, and you're tempted to tell yourself it's because their circumstances are much better or much easier than yours, remember the reality is that none of us know what most other people are going through in their personal lives, and none of us know what hurdles others are overcoming to achieve the things we wish we could achieve.

What we can be sure of is that everyone faces challenges. Everyone has something that they have to overcome to do whatever it is that everyone else dismisses as being easy for them.

When you look at someone else and think something isn't a challenge for them, the chances are that it only looks easy because of the time, effort and dedication they've put into it. Whether it's public speaking, dealing with customers, selling themselves or their business or keeping fit, the skills we aspire to have and the lives we aspire to live are achieved by others through hard work and commitment.

One of the biggest issues with ego is that, almost by stealth, it's there mainly to compensate for our absolutely huge, soul-crushing insecurity, otherwise known as caring too much what other people think.

Is that you? When you think about the possibility of doing something else, are you paralysed by the thought of what people on Facebook might think of you? Are you crippled by the chance that you might fail and everyone who you used to work with might laugh? What about your mates or your family, what would they think?

I've realised that not only are many, many people making decisions in their lives that make them miserable based largely on what other people think, but there's also a huge number of people who think that they are putting two fingers up to certain people in their lives by doing something solely to prove those other people wrong.

What a waste of a life.

The biggest issue I have with any of this is that for the vast majority of the time these decisions are being made based on *assumptions* about what other people think. Often, we are driven by something that hasn't actually ever been said but we act as though it's set in stone that it was.

Take my own story, for example. Nobody ever said to me that I had to be a lawyer, it was just something that I inferred from various sources and actions of others down the years.

If you are worried about what other people think, or are making decisions to prove someone wrong that are ultimately making you miserable, there's a very straightforward way to break free of that restraint.

Approach whoever it is that you're worried about and ask them if they would prefer you to carry on doing what you're doing and being miserable, or doing something else and being happy. If they are good people and say the latter you're instantly freed from your cage. If they say they'd rather you be miserable and carry on with whatever you're doing for some reason (probably their own insecurity), what type of people are they and why would you live your life in accordance with their rules?! Either way, you'll be free to make whatever decision makes you happiest.

In my experience, you'll find that all of the people you're worried about care far less about your life than you think anyway. As the famous quote goes:

"You probably wouldn't worry about what people think of you if you could know how seldom they do."

Depending on your character, there are two ways that you could take that thought. The first, which I wouldn't recommend, is that nobody cares about your life so what's the point in doing anything. But, the second, which in my view is the best way to live, is that if nobody really cares that much about what you're doing with your life (because, after all, they've got their own lives to worry about without worrying too much about yours), you are completely free to live in whatever way makes you as happy as possible, because it doesn't really affect anyone else anyway (provided, of course, that you aren't purposefully harming anyone else through your decisions).

Keeping down with the Smiths

This point also ties into something I like to refer to as *"Keeping down with the Smiths"*.

Never heard of it? I know, that's because I made it up. Good, isn't it?

I guess you've heard the expression *"Keeping up with the Joneses"*? If not, it refers to the idea that many people live their lives by reference to what their friends or neighbours are doing.

"Betty next door has bought a new car so I need to get one otherwise I'll look like I'm not doing as well as she is."

It's a big flag of insecurity and low self-esteem, yet for many people it will never be recognised as such. But I realised a few months ago that while keeping up with the Joneses is dangerous, keeping down with the Smiths might be even worse for you.

Keeping down with the Smiths, is what I see most people doing on the opposite side of *"Well, it's easy for Gary because ..."*, and it looks like this:

"I know I'm unhappy in my job, but I'm not as miserable as Steve."

"I know that my car's shit, but have you seen Julie's?"

"I know that I need to lose a few pounds, but I'm not as fat as Bill."

I'd go as far as saying that this is the excuse or rationalisation I hear most often as I walk through my daily life. And it's poisonous.

The thing is, whenever we're assessing our own lives and using others as a benchmark, we have two choices. We can either look up the hill and aspire to whatever it is those who are more advanced than us are doing, or we can look down the hill and comfort ourselves that we're not as bad as the people who aren't as advanced as us.

Every single person I've ever met, listened to or read about who is happy, fulfilled and successful in their life does two things:

1   they are content with their own place on the hill, neither envying those above them or pitying those below them; and

2   they are always looking up the hill, using the people who are more advanced than they are to inspire them to keep progressing, to keep growing and to keep moving forward in any one or more of a number of different areas.

All of the people I've ever met, listened to or read about who are miserable, unfulfilled or discontent with life and largely unsuccessful (including me a few years ago) do one or more of the following:

1   they use the people who they consider to be below them on the hill or not as advanced as them as reasons to justify why they aren't doing the things they want to do (*"I'm not as fat as Bill so I don't need to lose any weight"*);

2 they are perpetually dissatisfied with their own place in life, envying those more advanced than them and continually telling themselves stories about why it was easy for those people to get to where they are.

Importantly, that last point plagues rich people just as much as it plagues not-so-rich people, so if it applies to you it's unlikely to disappear simply by making more money.

You'll just find yourself dissatisfied while driving a Ferrari instead of a Skoda.

Next time you find yourself making an excuse for something because you think it's easier for someone else than it is for you, put your ego to one side for a second and see if you can think of anyone else who has more challenging circumstances than you and still achieves the same goal.

When it comes to changing careers, forget your excuses and ask whether anyone less fortunate than you has ever changed jobs or done something exceptional in similar or more challenging circumstances. When it comes to fitness and health, ask yourself whether there's anyone you know who is less fortunate than you or just as busy as you who still manages to stay in good shape and take care of themselves.

If it helps, when I decided to sell my law firm to try, again, to transform my life, I was over £150,000 in debt with credit cards and loans I'd used to supplement the business and my lifestyle for years. I was depressed, I had Crohn's disease and ankylosing spondylitis which kept me in agony every day and led to me feeling constantly lethargic.

But most people didn't know those things, so when I set up my online gambling business I still had to stand and listen to people who were actually in better positions than me saying things like *"oh, you're so lucky that you get to do that, I'd love to do that but I can't because [insert some bullshit excuse]"*. I know people who are sitting on hundreds of thousands of pounds yet still make excuses about why they can't do things that people with no money are doing.

Remember that there's always someone who can inspire you to do whatever it is you're telling yourself you can't do, whether it's someone you know who works long hours but still makes time to go to the gym, someone who overcame shyness to become a great salesperson, someone who made tough decisions to change their career, their business or their life for the better, or someone who simply stopped watching TV for six months to create more time to work on a side business.

Instead of making excuses, find someone who has done what you want to do and find out how they did it. Put your ego to one side and stop convincing yourself that your life is so much more difficult than everyone else's.

Exercise

As a quick exercise, just write down on a piece of paper all of the things that you've been using as excuses for not doing whatever it is you want to do, then ask yourself whether there is anyone less fortunate than you – or in the same position – who has achieved what you want to achieve.

If you can't think of anyone, do a search on Google and see what comes up. I guarantee that if you search for how to do whatever it is you want to do you'll find it. And I also guarantee that if you keep searching for all of the reasons you can't do the same thing, you'll find them, too.

You find in life whatever you look for, so if you tell yourself *"I can't do this"* then your brain will tell you all the ways you can't do it, but if you ask yourself, or ask Google, *"how can I do this?"*, you'll find as many answers as you can handle.

Whenever I find myself even contemplating making an excuse to justify something I'm not doing, I think of someone like Kyle Maynard.

If you haven't heard of Kyle, he was born with a rare condition known as congenital amputation that left him with arms that end at the elbows and legs that end near his knees. Despite that, he became the first quadruple amputee to reach the summit of Mount Kilimanjaro and Mount Aconcagua without the aid of prosthetics.

I'll say that again in case you missed it.

He climbed Mount Kilimanjaro and Mount Aconcagua with no arms and legs.

Whenever I think of a measly excuse for not doing something, I think of Kyle. If he can do that, what's your excuse?

As the famous Henry Ford quote goes, whether you think you can or think you can't, you're right.

The Blame Game

If Kyle's example isn't enough to get you beyond your excuses, it's probably because the beauty of the ego is that it's all-powerful. It's like the massive, evil eye in *The Lord of The Rings*, watching over everyone and being a general nuisance.

Wikipedia says that the psychoanalysis definition of ego is *"the part of the mind that mediates between the conscious and the unconscious and is responsible for reality testing and a sense of personal identity"*.

Fancy.

I like to see it as the little bellend inside my head trying to tell me to do things that I shouldn't be doing and which aren't in my best interests, and stopping me from doing things that are. Again, I'm not sure if my local dialect translates to your part of the world, but *'bellend'* is basically *'dick head'* with a bit less edge. It's something you'd call your mate if he was annoying you while still acknowledging that he's your friend.

"Stop doing that, you bellend" is the type of thing I say to my ego these days (and also something that my mates have said to me for years). He seems to respond quite well to it so you might want to give it a try.

If that doesn't work and your ego is persuading you that your problems were all caused by someone other than you and, therefore, they're beyond your control, it's worthwhile breaking them down one at a time. Pick whichever is the first thing you hate about your life that springs to mind. Don't think about it too much, just go with the first one that pops in to your head when you allow yourself to think of the things you dislike most.

Got one?

Okay, now for the fun part.

Who is it that you currently blame for that problem? Is it your current partner? Your kids? Your mum or dad? How about your boss or the company you work for? Or is it not a person but a thing? Maybe you're telling yourself you just don't have the time.

If there are other people involved in your blame game, the key is to break down precisely what it is that they're doing, or have done, that is preventing you from doing what you say you'd do if it wasn't for them.

By way of example, a few months ago I reached breaking point in my marriage. We'd been going through shit for years, with a combination of my business ventures causing unnecessary stress to our relationship and my wife's jobs over the years bringing misery into the house. Looking back, it was a recipe for disaster and I'm amazed we lasted as long as we did.

For the purposes of this chapter, though, the key is how I was behaving in the last 12 months before I finally moved out.

From the driven, enthusiastic, eager entrepreneur I'd been in the years before, I'd become a lethargic, downtrodden (some might even say lazy) inhabitant of my own house. I'd told myself a story that I needed to decompress from all of the years of stress and strain on my body and mind (which was partly true), and had taken to having frequent afternoon naps while still doing enough consultancy work to pay the bills each month. During that period, my wife was still working in a hugely stressful job and it didn't sit well with her that I would be taking a nap on the couch at 4pm while she was tearing her hair out with work.

On top of that, because her work involved numerous things that I could help with, I'd find myself asking about what was happening then getting involved to try to help to fix things or resolve problems. I found that it started taking up more and more of my time, which led to me doing fewer of the things that I needed to do to move my own projects forward.

Over and over again, we would have tense conversations, sometimes full-blown arguments, in which I would blame my wife for the fact that I couldn't get any momentum behind the things I was working on because of her and her stupid, stressful job interfering with what I was doing.

My argument was that because her work was so negative and stressful, it drained me of all of my magical energy and led to me needing to lie on the couch watching Netflix during the evenings instead of doing anything productive.

But that was all bollocks.

Looking back, I had no one to blame but myself. If I'd really wanted to get work done that wasn't getting done, I had numerous options open to me to do just that. I could have refused to get involved in her work, I could have started working away from the house during the day or I could have done what I've been doing lately, and what I'd done for so many years before, which was working between 7pm and 4am instead of sleeping or watching mindless TV that I wasn't even interested in. Ultimately, I also could have left the relationship earlier.

The reality is this. We find the time and energy to do the things we really want to do. If something comes up in your life that you absolutely must do, you'll find a way of doing it. Whether you need to get an extra credit card, borrow money from someone or lose a night's sleep, when the motivation is right we're all capable of pulling off minor miracles.

Can you think of anything you've done in the past that you wanted so badly you just made it happen regardless of the consequences? A weekend away with your friends that you couldn't really afford? A meal out with your partner which you didn't really have the money for? Maybe someone's party you didn't have time for but managed to make it work by getting the kids looked after by someone in the family, or presents you bought for your children for Christmas despite not really being able to afford them?

Whatever it was, when the motivation was right you got it done and you made the tough decisions that were necessary.

And that's why the blame game has to stop if you want to move forward into a happier and more fulfilling life. Whatever it is that you are blaming for your current inaction you need to banish it, take responsibility and figure out how you can move forward in spite of whatever the challenge is.

Exercise

To help you to do that, use the table below to write down the left-hand side all of the excuses you can think of for not doing whatever it is that you want to do. Then, in the next column, write down all of the people and things that you are blaming in those excuses and be brutally honest about it. If you're blaming your beautiful, innocent little children for you not doing the things you want to do with your life, make sure you put that down. Don't worry about feeling like a bad person, that's part of the process and you'll quickly figure out how not to blame them so all will be well with the world again.

Finally, in the last column, write down all of the ways that, if you really put your mind to it, those excuses would just fall away. Don't allow any restrictions to stop you writing anything in that column, again being brutally honest. By that, I mean if you're blaming your partner for stopping you doing something you want to do, you should write in the last column *"leave my partner"* or *"move out temporarily*". I know you might recoil at that comment, but it's important that you write down all of the options available to you. Again, if you'd like to download the table to use, you can find it at *www.changeyourcareer.org/rationalisation.*

Excuse	People or things being blamed	Options
1.		
2.		
3.		
4.		
5.		
6.		
7.		
8.		
9.		
10.		

After you've listed your options, you simply need to select which one or more of them you could take to overcome whatever excuse you are currently relying on.

To give one final, less intense, example from my own life of general excuse being made, a good mate of mine said to me years after I'd set up the law firm and the online gambling business that it amazed him how I did both of those things because he wouldn't even know where to start, so could never have done it himself. His excuse was that he didn't know as much as me, despite also being a highly qualified lawyer who had been to law school and is now a partner at a major international practice.

"You would know," I said.

"Honestly, mate, I wouldn't."

"If I put a gun to your head right now and said figure out how to start a gambling business, what would you do?"

"Ha, I'd probably just type 'how to start a gambling business' into Google and go from there."

"That's what I did, mate."

We live in a time in which anything you want to do is a Google search or YouTube video away. You can learn to do anything you want to do, as long as you're willing to put the work in.

The biggest mistake is overestimating everyone else and underestimating yourself.

You are capable of whatever you put your mind to unless, of course, you're just afraid …

"The hero and the coward both feel the same thing, but the hero uses his fear, projects it onto his opponent, while the coward runs. It's the same thing, fear, but it's what you do with it that matters."

–CUS D'AMATO
(MIKE TYSON'S TRAINER/MANAGER)

Part 3 – Addiction, Family and Fear

Fear

This could be my favourite part of my favourite child. It's the little chubby cheeks on its little face that make you just want to give them a squeeze and grin all day long.

In my opinion, fear is at the root of everything that's bad in the world. It's the cause of wars, of discrimination, of terrorism and, on a smaller level from a global perspective but no less important for us, it's the main thing holding people back in their lives and keeping them imprisoned in miserable, unfulfilling careers.

Now, the problem is that the topic of fear is enough to fill an entire book in itself, as well as a full video course and week-long live seminar, all of which I'm working on. So, I'll give you the high-level summary in order to avoid overloading you with too much information at once. If after reading this you might be interested in a more thorough exploration of the topic, please go to www.changeyourcareer.org/fear and let me know.

For the purposes of this expedition to the next phase of your life, I need to take you back to something I mentioned to you earlier that I said might have caused some recoiling in your seat depending on your views.

Therapy.

Here's the thing. Through exploring various issues that had been building up throughout the past 38 years of my life, including intermittent anger explosions, general dissatisfaction and extreme tension both psychological and physical, I made a breakthrough that was mind blowing in its level of unexpectedness.

I was afraid.

Now, I feel as though you know quite a bit about me at this stage of the quest, but it's worth pointing a few things out if they're not already apparent.

I did not at any point in my adult life consider myself to be afraid of anything. Not only am I from a city where the men pride themselves on being able to look after themselves physically in a very old-fashioned *"who are you looking at?"* kind of way, but from a more emotional and psychological perspective I would always describe myself as being fearless.

To put it into perspective, I used to be afraid of heights so, in order to rid myself of the one fear that I felt was holding me back in a very minor way, I decided to climb over the top of the Sydney Harbour Bridge when I was travelling after university. Not climbing over by myself, obviously, I'm not a complete lunatic, but on the organised expedition that has made someone somewhere an incredible amount of money.

This is an example of how I lived my life, facing challenges and fears head on, quitting a well-paid job when it no longer served me, setting up companies I had no prior knowledge of and generally not backing down to anything the world had to throw at me.

If you'd asked me 12 months ago, I would have told you with great certainty that I was afraid of nothing. But then one day, sitting in a therapist's room in a city centre office in Liverpool, I had a total epiphany. By examining my childhood, my relationships with my parents and wider family, and my relationship with my wife, I discovered, much to my surprise, that I was actually pretty insecure about loads of things, and had fairly low self-esteem.

I don't know about you, but it wasn't a twist in the story I was expecting at this stage of my life.

It turns out that all of my anger issues, in particular, were built on a foundation of being afraid of not being good enough, not being lovable enough and not being worthy enough.

I know, right?

It blew my socks off when it happened. But after I realised, something incredible happened. It was as though as soon as the curtain had been pulled down and I could see the truth about myself, I could also see the truth about everyone else.

It was like the scene from *The Matrix* when Neo is given the option to take the red pill or the blue one. I, like him, took the red one, and now all I can see all around me is fear running amok.

A perfect example happened just a week after my own personal revelation.

* * *

I'm standing in the back garden of my house in Formby, in the northern suburbs of Liverpool, with my dad who has come to mow the lawns. At this stage of my life I am more than capable of mowing my own lawns but, as you know, my dad is retired and likes to keep himself busy, so I think it's a nice way of us spending a bit of father and son time together doing something he enjoys.

It's a bright, sunny day with clear blue skies. My garden is long and thin, stretching out from the back of a semi-detached brick-built house with grass running the length of its 30 metres. There are trees down the right-hand side as you look from the house, a patio near the back door with a wicker table and chair set and a shed half way down on the left-hand side that has been turned into an outside working space by the landlord.

My dad is setting up his lawn mower and my eight-month old, white West Highland Terrier puppy, Tilly, has come out to say hello to her granddad who she absolutely adores. He's the only person she knows who has a greenhouse in his back garden with tomatoes growing, which she is mesmerised by, and a compost heap behind his shed which is heaven for a dog who loves to bury anything she can in massive piles of mud.

I've said I'll do some weeding further up the garden to make myself useful while he's mowing, and ask whether he's happy for Tilly to stay outside or whether he'd rather I put her in the house. He says breezily that she's fine where she is, so I turn my back and head off away from the two of them.

A few seconds later, after my dad has started the mower and its motor is whirring away, I can hear Tilly barking her little head off and making a right old commotion. Within another few seconds, I hear my dad shout out angrily and I turn around to see Tilly jumping up at him, with him shouting down the garden for me to put the bloody dog inside because she's just bitten him. I walk down towards them both and he's clearly annoyed with her for attacking him.

And that's when I see it for the first time.

We're looking at the exact same scene, and where my dad sees an angry dog attacking him, I see a frightened little puppy scared of a lawn mower and jumping up for help.

And now I see it everywhere.

You see a woman ranting and raving about her boss and I see a little girl who's petrified that she might lose her job when she's got a family to keep. You see an angry man shouting at his kids in the supermarket and I see a scared little boy who has no idea what to do and is desperate for some help. You see a fight between high-powered executives and I see kids scared witless about the uncertainty surrounding the future of their companies.

I can feel it in you right now, with all of those little things and some of those big things racing through your mind, each one based on insecurity and fear.

I watched a great video a few days ago by the modern-day philosopher Alain de Botton, who I love, talking about the problem with adults being that we have adult bodies. If, as would be more appropriate, we were all still running around in the bodies of five-year-olds, we'd be much nicer and much more compassionate to each other about the issues we are all secretly carrying around that no one else can see and often we don't even know about.

Does my wife love me? Why do I feel so different to other people? Will I be able to pay the mortgage this month? Am I a fraud? Can everyone else see that I haven't got a fucking clue what I'm doing?

And they're just a selection of my own fears from over the past 10 years.

What are yours? As you just sit for a few moments and contemplate all of this, again being completely honest with yourself, what are the things that pass through your mind? When you can't sleep at night, what are the thoughts keeping you awake?

Exercise

Write them all down. Just get a big, blank piece of paper and start writing down as many as you can. Let your hand go into autopilot and don't think about it. Allow your answers to come from your gut, your heart and your soul.

It's important that you don't allow your ego to get involved in this process, because it will immediately begin to tell you that your deepest, darkest fears or insecurities are not even real and you don't need to worry about them one bit.

Just remember to say the magic line *"stop doing that, you bellend"* and continue listening to the real you.

Answer these two questions with whatever is the first thing that pops out when you read them.

1   What is the thing you like least about yourself?

2   What one thing about you would you hate the world to know?

All done?

Seeing as we're doing this remotely without being able to discuss it in any detail you might have struggled to get anything useful or anything that you didn't already know, which is fine. At this point it's more important to try to identify as many root cause issues that are or have been holding you back in the past, so whatever you've come up with is great. It's always easier to do these exercises in a live setting, but at this moment in time books don't let us do that.

The challenge now is to take whatever fears you've identified and do the "why?" process from Chapter 4 to get as far down into the root of them as you possibly can. I'll warn you in advance that if you're doing this exercise completely openly and honestly with yourself, without holding back or letting your ego intellectualise anything, you might well end up in childhood territory figuring out the root causes of all of your fears or in experiences from your later years that have scarred you on some subconscious level since they took place.

Once you've identified them, it's time to overcome them.

Before we dig into the power of the imagination when it comes to overcoming fear, the most straightforward way to rid yourself of the things that you're afraid of is to analyse each one and think of all of the ways in which you could make the fear go away. This technique works better for fears like *"I don't know if I can afford to pay the mortgage if I change my job"* than it does for *"I'm absolutely petrified of bananas"*.

For the former, an example of a possible solution is to find a way to guarantee that your mortgage can be paid regardless of you changing jobs. Let's say that your mortgage or rent is £800 per month, you either need to save up enough money to make sure that you have a pot of cash available to pay it for a specified number of months (basically however long you think it will take for your new career to generate income), or you could find a way of guaranteeing that you have enough money to pay your essential (non-negotiable) outgoings every month through another source of income (for example, you could go part time in your current job while transitioning to something new).

When thinking of potential solutions to the things that you're afraid of, treat it as a freethinking brainstorming exercise in which there are no stupid answers. You'd be amazed how often something that starts as a crazy idea ends up being a brilliant solution.

If you're struggling with any of this, a few examples of common fears and possible solutions are set out below. You can also contact me using the email address at the end of the book if you have a fear that you can't seem to get past, and I'll additionally talk later about joining a group of like-minded people who will all be able to help each other through these processes at *www.changeyourcareer.org/tribe*.

Common Fear

I will fail.

Possible Solutions / Thoughts

Define what you think that failure looks like specifically. If you are setting up a new business, set yourself small, achievable goals that all build up to a bigger goal over time, rather than setting a target that is likely to lead to failure.

Remember that everyone fails, even the greatest entrepreneurs, athletes and pop stars. In fact, the one thing that everyone on the planet who has ever tried anything has in common is that they have failed repeatedly at many, many things. Failure is just part of the journey, and the only true failure is giving up. Everything else is just experience.

Common Fear

People will laugh at me.

Possible Solutions / Thoughts

Which people? If you're worried about what friends, family or Facebook people might think, you can do as suggested in Chapter 6, part 2 and ask them what they do think instead of worrying about what they might think. You'll probably find that most people will be supportive if they know it's something you really want to do because you are really miserable in your life. If they aren't supportive, maybe they aren't people whose opinions you should care about and, instead, find people who will support you every step of the way (see Chapter 9 or visit *www.changeyourcareer. org/tribe* for more information). See also the section headed "Be careful whose advice you listen to" at the end of this chapter.

Common Fear

I'm not good enough.

Possible Solutions / Thoughts

Not good enough at what? Be specific about what you think your shortcomings are then think of all of the ways in which you either can do the things you worry about or ways in which you could overcome the problem. In general terms, you are good enough to do whatever you want to do in life, but you might not be able to do everything that you need to do in order to achieve your goals without help. Which is absolutely fine. I can't do everything that I need to, so I outsource the things that I can't do to people who can. Be realistic and positive. There's a difference between telling yourself that you're generally not good enough to change your life, which is not true, and telling yourself that you aren't very good at one or more things that you think you need to be able to do. Some of the most successful people in the world have reached their positions in life because they are able to identify their shortcomings and work with other people who make up for those things. Focus on your strengths, not your weaknesses, and things will become much easier.

Common Fear

I can't afford to lose my job.

Possible Solutions / Thoughts

Go through the process of counting the numbers in Chapter 5 to calculate exactly how much your job is worth to you each month from a financial perspective. Once you have that number, brainstorm all of the ways that, in the worst-case scenario of you losing your job and the associated income, you could still pay your essential living costs. For example, in the very worst-case scenario, could you rent out your house and move in with parents, other family members or friends? Could you get short term temporary work that would plug the gap until you figured out what you want to do? Once we identify the worst-case scenario and account for it, it's often not as bad as we first feared.

It's important to remember when thinking about this topic that fear is felt by *everyone* or, at least, everyone who isn't a complete psychopath. Never look at people who have done something you would like to do and think that they weren't ever afraid. Everyone's afraid. As Cus D'Amato says, it's what you choose to do with it that counts.

Don't let fear hold you back from creating the career and life that you have always dreamed of. Once you've delved deep into the root causes of your fear, you might find that most of it exists only in your …

Imagination

Again, it's impossible to take you through the entirety of the exercises needed to rid yourself of all fears in one chapter of one book, especially when the subject matter is so complex. I don't want to overload you too much when the purpose of the book is to transform your career or life rather than just focusing on getting rid of fears.

So, we'll focus on the most important antidote to most fears: controlling your imagination.

In this context, by 'imagination' I mean the stories that we tell ourselves during every minute of every day. I mean the things that are running through your mind even as you read this book, and the places you drift off to every time your brain wanders somewhere other than the page you're meant to be reading.

The stories we tell ourselves are possibly the most important part of our lives, because those stories are, ultimately, who we believe ourselves to be.

Going back to my earlier example, for years I've told myself the story that I'm fearless. It was a story I'd built up unconsciously to the point that my ego believed it absolutely. Looking back, though, I always knew in my gut that it wasn't true, I just chose over the decades to bury those feelings and to rely on what my brain wanted to convince itself of.

In previous stages of my life I told myself that I was invincible, that I was different and that I was alone. It's taken some real beatings from the universe to show me in no uncertain terms that those things are not true, which I am extremely thankful for. Now I'm able to tell myself the far healthier stories that I'm vulnerable, just like everyone else, and connected to others in more ways than I can remember.

And that's where the imagination is so important, because nothing has actually changed other than the stories I tell myself.

What stories do you tell yourself? What character have you created to deal with your fears and insecurities so that no one knows about them?

My character was a cocky, often arrogant, egotistical, self-assured entrepreneur who was going to take over the world. He displayed many signs of narcissism and used his armour to protect him from having to look inwardly at all of the weaknesses and flaws that existed in the real operating system on which he was running, leading to anger management issues and poor health.

It was like in *Superman III* when the hero turns dark and starts using his powers for evil. Only I still couldn't fly or shoot laser beams out of my eyes (as you can tell I'm extremely bitter about not getting any real super powers at any point in my life).

Fortunately for me, that character has now started to get written out of the soap opera of my life and replaced by the original version that existed when I was a little boy. A calm, peaceful, friendly person who just wants to help others to live better lives. Don't get me wrong, there's still some way to go before I manage to shut the ego up on a more regular basis, and it's almost impossible once he's persuaded me to have more than four or five drinks, but it's a work in progress that's better than it was before.

It's not only the stories we tell ourselves that are important, though, it's also the stories that we've been told for years and believed to be true but which are absolutely nonsense.

Let me give you an example that might seem daft but illustrates the point perfectly.

A couple of years ago when combing my hair one morning, I had a really strange moment. I looked at my hairline and could have sworn that it was receding. I started pulling back my fringe so that I could inspect more closely, and it seemed as though my hair was getting thinner.

But that couldn't possibly be true.

Day after day it was playing on my mind, to the point where I decided after a few months to get an expert opinion. I went to see a hair loss expert who took one look at me, pinned the front of my hair back and confirmed, absolutely, that I was losing my hair.

It was another moment when the walls started tumbling all around me and I realised that I'd been listening to another lie my entire life and had never questioned it. I called my older sister and started chatting to her and laughing about what had happened and what I'd realised had gone on in my head. Her response was perfect.

"It's mad, you know, sis. I just always thought I'd always have a good head of hair, so it has properly taken me aback that I might be going bald."

"That's funny."

"Do you know why I always thought I'd never go bald? Do you remember what mum always said as we were growing up?"

"Of course. She's always told us that 'the men in this family have great heads of hair'!"

We both burst out laughing. As I started listing the men in our family, there was one after the next who was either completely bald or, at best, had thinning or receding hair. Probably no different to any other collection of men in any family in the world.

When I told my mum, her first reaction was to declare that I was wrong, that all the men had great heads of hair. Even when I started describing my cousin, who is bald, and my uncle, her brother, whose hairline starts at the crown of his head, she just couldn't accept it. In fact, when I told her that her brother was bald, her exact reply was *"He. Is. Not."*

I realised then that she'd told herself the story her whole life that all of the men in the family had great hair, which was no doubt a story told to her by her mum, and her mum before that. It was so powerful that she could no longer see the reality.

That story was told to me and my sister so often when we were growing up that we both still remember it now at 38 and 40 years old. Another story that had been told to me so many times that I'd started telling it to myself and believing it when it couldn't have been further from the truth.

Whatever stories you've been telling yourself, go back to when you were a little kid and remember how it felt back then compared to whoever you tell yourself you are now. That little person is much more likely to be the real you than the character you've built up over the years.

And whatever stories you've been told by others, question them, challenge them and figure out which are true and which are absolute nonsense.

Past, Future and Now

In addition to the stories you tell yourself, the other element of the imagination that is crucial to this process when it comes to ridding yourself of fear is its ability to convince you that things are real that don't actually exist.

To illustrate, think of something right now that you're afraid of. It could be heights, a spider, your partner leaving you or losing your job, it doesn't matter for the purposes of the exercise.

Got something?

Okay. Now focus on whatever it is. Picture it in your mind as clearly as you can. Look at the scene through your own eyes. If you're scared of heights, put yourself at the top of whatever structure you would be most scared of being on. If it's your partner leaving you, imagine the images as they walk out the door for the last time. Go there. Imagine it as vividly as you can.

What can you feel when you really focus on it? What can you see? What can you feel? Is it cold or warm? Are there any smells in the scene, or any sounds? Make the colours brighter, make any smells more pungent and the sounds louder. Focus on the feelings. Intensify them. Turn them up and up. Double the sounds and the intensity of the colours then double them again. What's happening? Can you feel your heart rate increase? Is your breathing getting faster? Do you feel uncomfortable? Maybe you're even starting to sweat a little bit.

If any of that happened just allow yourself to come back to the page and let the images in your mind fade away to nothing. Let the colours wash away so that it's just a white screen in your mind and turn off any sounds or smells that were there.

If there was any level of discomfort, increased heart rate or breathing they should now have returned to normal. You're safe and comfortable right where you are.

If you did feel any heightened emotions, notice how everything that just happened was all in your imagination. You're really just reading a book. Yet our brains can convince our bodies of all kinds of madness when the situation suits, and this is the danger. It's no different to when we see something frightening on TV and we feel afraid even though we know nothing is going to jump out of the TV and hurt us, or when we feel queasy watching a video of someone looking over the edge of a cliff.

Ultimately, whatever you're scared of that is holding you back in your life exists mainly in your imagination. It's either something from the past that you are reliving over and over again for no particular reason, or it's something that you think *might* happen in the future which you're torturing yourself about when you can't even be sure it will come about.

When we start to worry about anything, if we just bring ourselves back to the current moment, take 10 big, deep breaths, let our shoulders relax and the tension across our face and back melt away, all of a sudden whatever it was that we were thinking about seems less stressful.

And this is the key to transforming your life and escaping the fears that are holding you back.

Once you've identified what those fears are and analysed them to break them down into their specific parts, make sure that you are not paralysed by an imaginary future or an image from the past that can no longer hurt you.

To give you a very basic Neuro Linguistic Programming (NLP) technique to use whenever you find yourself thinking of something that makes you anxious, angry, fearful or any other negative emotion that is holding you back, go through the following steps and notice how the thought in your imagination completely changes.

1   Think of whatever it is that's creating a challenge for you.

2   Notice what you can see when you picture the image in your mind.

3   Are you looking at the scene as if you're looking through your own eyes or can you see yourself in the picture?

4   However you're looking at it, just imagine jumping backwards out of your body so that you're now looking at the same scene as though it's on a TV in front of you.

5   Focus on the colours and any sounds, smells or feelings.

6   Now just turn them all down as though you are turning the dials on a TV and slowly reducing everything. Notice how the colours slowly fade to black and white, how any sounds and smells disappear and the feelings you used to attach to the thought melt away.

7   Imagine the TV slowly drifting away from you, getting smaller and smaller as it disappears with the image on it until it's become nothing more than a black spot on a big white screen, miles away from you in the distance.

Does the thought of whatever it was still fill you with as much negative emotion as it did before? If not, try using the above technique with any negative memories or thoughts that you have.

Remember, everything that is in your mind is just a story that you are telling yourself, and it's possible to change that story if you really want to.

*Maybe it's time to let
the old ways die
It takes a lot to
change a man
Hell, it takes
a lot to try
Maybe it's time to let
the old ways die*

Jason Isbell / Bradley Cooper
Maybe it's time
(A Star is Born)

Family and Addiction

I'll say up front that I feel a little bit bad for including this section when I know for sure that it simply cannot be done justice in a few pages. There are reams of research, studies and books that cover these wide topics, which I'm digging into more and more as the weeks progress, so I include reference only to make you aware of the issue and allow you to look further into it if you so wish.

This, I'm afraid, is another *"look at yourself properly in the mirror and be absolutely petrified"* part of the book.

Family

My current reading of things is that our general psychology, ultimately, leads back largely to our family of origin or, to be more specific, usually our parents or the people who raised us. It is fairly likely that my next book will be solely focussed on this topic because I am forever in search of the ultimate root cause of all problems, and I think I might well have realised that our families are exactly that. Whether or not you think you were brought up in a normal, loving family, if you've felt the need to buy this book there's a reasonable chance that you are at least a little bit messed up from your childhood without having any inkling that is the case.

For the purposes of our work here, though, we'll focus on the vulnerabilities and weaknesses that you are likely to have that might be holding you back from making the step that you need to make.

For once we get to look in the mirror properly by first looking at everyone else. Grab that piece of paper and pen again ...

Exercise

I want you to spend five minutes writing down all of the things that you absolutely hate in other people. All of the things that you despise, that wind you up, that get under your skin. Anything that you feel is a real core belief of yours, something that you believe to be part of you and that you feel completely righteous about.

To give you an example, my two big ones were that I hated hypocrites and could not stand disloyalty. By way of other examples, someone very close to me has a huge issue with people being overweight and someone else can't stand manipulative people. They are so striking in their beliefs that they refer to these things constantly.

Obviously, this isn't going to be a very nice list, but do it openly and honestly as you have with all of the other exercises. You can burn it afterwards so that no one else sees it.

* * *

Are you finished?

Okay, now for the tough part. There is a very real possibility (it could even be a strong probability), that whatever you've written down is something that you hate because it's actually a part of you; that deep inside your subconscious you have been suppressing something, possibly for so long that you can't even recognise it anymore, and it eats away at you slowly every day.

For my part, I had a sudden moment of realisation when telling stories about my past that the reason I couldn't stand hypocrites and that I hated people being disloyal was because I had a key story in my past that showed me as being both disloyal and, therefore, a hypocrite.

I'd just told myself over the years that my actions at the time were justified, but the problem the ego has is that while it can convince your daft brain that something is true, your clever subconscious knows all along that it isn't, and the subconscious has a tendency to remember these things and to manifest them in weird and wonderful ways as a twisted little trick on your life.

Do you look at other people and see insecurity everywhere? There's a reasonable chance that you're insecure as well but have suppressed that side of you so much that you no longer recognise it. Do you see manipulation everywhere you look? You guessed it, you're probably a little manipulator. Or wherever you glance there are selfish people who you can't stand? Yep, it's probably that you're selfish and can't see it. Don't get me wrong, you probably aren't incorrect in your assessment of others, but I like to think this is where the playground line *"takes one to know one"* comes from. It's far easier for us to spot things in other people that are in us but we can't see in ourselves.

If you take a step back from your own life and think about things that have been said to you over the years, maybe by people when they were drunk, maybe by someone who didn't like you or maybe during an argument with your partner. Did you just dismiss those comments? Did you allow your ego to justify in your own mind why it's not really true?

I know that I've done both of those things.

Do you ever find yourself saying lines like, *"I know I'm not perfect, but ... "*, *"I know I can be like X, but ... "* or when someone says something about you that you don't like but which you see in them, you find yourself uttering the line *"That's the pot calling the kettle black"*.

The problem is that we focus on the fact that the pot is black without acknowledging that the kettle is, too.

If any of the above things have happened in your life, the key is to pause before rushing past. It's really difficult to do because it results in us having to look closely at the darkest parts of our personalities that our egos are distracting us from for a reason: they're not very nice parts. But if you can sit with the discomfort and allow yourself to reflect on what someone said to you that you didn't like and all the ways in which they might actually be right, you will have a chance to rid yourself of those negative traits once and for all.

If you find yourself saying you're not perfect in passing before going on to focus on the faults of your partner or someone else who it's easier to focus on, just catch yourself and really think about all of the ways in which you're not perfect and what you could do to rectify those things that would make your life and the lives of the people around you better.

Saying *"I know I'm not perfect, but ..."* implies that you think that you are very close to being perfect, whereas whoever you're about to talk about is far from it. If you do that I've got some bad news for you, which is that you're probably very far from being perfect, just like everyone else. I hate the idea of perfectionism anyway (more on that later), so it's no bad thing to accept that we're all flawed human beings and to acknowledge the things that we need to work on.

When doing this, you might find that the things that you hate in others are also things that you dislike in your own family, possibly your parents, which is where this all ties back into your origins.

I found this process really painful, because it led to me realising that so many things in my past were not as I thought they were. It led me to realise that I had often not been as good a person as I previously thought, which was incredibly tough to take.

But, on the other side of it all, it meant that I could start, for the first time in my adult life, to begin to rid myself of those negative personality traits that other people could see but that I was blind to, freeing me to become happier and more fulfilled in my work and my life in general.

The reality is that all of these issues tend to start in our childhood, so we can be kind to ourselves and realise that our negative character traits are just our subconscious minds trying to find ways for our needs to be met which aren't being met otherwise. If we can identify what they are and why they're happening, we can make sure that our needs are being met in a more positive and productive way, which removes the need for our subconscious to find a way to make sure that they're met on our behalf.

As an aside, it's worth noting this doesn't mean all of our problems are the fault of our family. These issues tend to go back through generations, so whoever raised you was just doing the best they could with what they'd been taught growing up. It's important to remember that and to be compassionate with ourselves and with those around us when dealing with these topics.

One of the main problems in your life right now, which has probably been a problem for a number of years if you've decided to buy this book, is that you aren't growing. You've been stale for years. You went from year after year during your younger life learning new things and achieving new goals, to living a repetitive life doing nothing new. And without growth we slowly die. We need to grow to thrive. While it might sound crazy, going deep inside yourself and dealing with these things will, if nothing else, help you to grow in ways you couldn't imagine.

The main reason I raise this in the context of this book, however, is that it links to something even more destructive that is likely to be holding you back and preventing you from doing whatever it is you're desperate to do.

Addictions

Again, I appreciate before we go any further that this is far from a definitive piece on this complex subject, and I am speaking largely from my own experience bearing in mind that I am only just starting out on the path to knowledge and expertise in this area. Forgive me then if you feel it isn't 100 per cent accurate (we should, after all, be willing to accept that we don't ever know everything and also be prepared to check whether what we think or what we read is true).

So, here's what I've found.

The gaps in my soul that existed because of the things I had suppressed for so many years and had, instead, projected onto those around me, were ultimately being filled by addictions.

Addictions are the things we use to numb the pain of day to day life because it's not as fulfilling as we would like it to be. We use them to help us to get through the days, the weeks or the months, until 5pm on Friday or our two week summer holiday.

Now, when I say "addictions" you might immediately think of serious drugs, alcoholism, sex or some other headline grabber, and you'd be right to do so. But the real problem in this is that our addictions go far deeper and far wider than problems that society has deemed to be the pariahs of the addiction world. In fact, in some ways you're lucky if you've managed to pick up one of the black listed addictions because you're more likely to have been forced to do something about it.

The real problems lie in the stealth addictions. The ones society not only tolerates, but encourages. The ones everyone has, so nobody questions.

Let me expand.

Do you ever come in from work, pick up the remote control and turn on the TV without thinking about it? Are you ever sitting on your couch late at night and scrolling through the channels hoping to find something to watch, before landing on a movie you've seen 147 times that is halfway through and deciding to stay up until 2am to watch the end of it? Do you ever find yourself buying things in the shops that you don't actually need? Maybe new tea towels for the kitchen or clothes for the kids? Do you sit mindlessly scrolling through social media channels for chunks of the day? Or eating food when you aren't hungry even though you already feel bad about the weight you've gained and how lethargic you feel? Do you throw yourself into work, powering through long hours? Do you have an alcoholic drink every night? Do you go to the gym obsessively every day? Do you find yourself not being able to say no to a chocolate bar, incessantly complaining about or judging others, picking up your phone to check for messages when nothing has beeped, obsessing about your relationship or watching porn every day?

If so, you're almost certainly an addict.

You might have chosen something that society is fairly happy with as being your drug of choice, and going to the gym every day is without doubt better than taking heroin, but you are an addict nevertheless and it is likely to be having some negative impact on your life, even if that impact is only that it distracts you from dealing with the real root of the problem.

From a work and relationship perspective, it could be one of the key reasons why you find it impossible to leave in search of something more fulfilling. Addictions work at their very core on the psychology of intermittent rewards. Think of a slot machine in a casino, and how in addition to all of the flashing lights and enticing music, they pay out prizes on what seems to be a completely random basis.

The fact that you don't know when the reward for your behaviour is coming is the very thing that keeps you hooked. It's possibly the same with the job you hate or the relationship you just can't seem to leave. You'll be getting towards the point of thinking that it's time to cut the strings when, all of a sudden, something positive happens that makes you think that there might be hope and that things will improve in the future. But then everything goes back to normal.

It's the intermittent reward that keeps you hooked because you're an addict, so resolving the root cause of your addiction is the best way to ensure you can rid this curse from your life, because unless you cure the root cause you will only manage to move from one addiction to another.

We are all rats in cages pressing levers hoping to get some food, having no idea when the food will be dispensed so we just keep pressing the lever. Not only do we need to stop pressing the lever, but it's important that we make it so that we have no desire to press the lever by filling the gap in ourselves that causes the addiction in the first place.

Getting into the real nitty-gritty of this topic is beyond the scope of this book, but it's worth talking about and identifying because if you are able to solve whatever the root cause of your addiction is, whatever it is that you're trying to numb the pain of, you will have a much greater chance of freeing your mind and body to do the things you want and need to do in order to move forward. If nothing else, removing an addiction is likely to free up a whole load of time that you could be using far more productively elsewhere (even if that's by not being hung-over and out of action every Saturday and Sunday, or not watching TV every night).

Part 4 – Be careful whose advice you listen to

This is a short but very important topic needed to address something that could well have been holding you back from changing your life before now without you realising it, and it ties in to my origins story.

I have over the years listened to the advice of many, many people, including close members of my own family. It's important to say that I do not blame anyone in my past for giving me the advice that they gave with the best of intentions based on their own life experiences. After all, that's all any of us can do if someone asks us for advice, isn't it?

But something I've learned through all of my years of experience wandering down the long and winding road I've travelled, is that the vast majority of advice we receive we should just allow to wash over us without doing much more than acknowledging its existence.

There are even books I've read that I consider to have been life changing which contain parts that I have completely ignored because they didn't suit what I was looking to do with my life. I would urge you to do the same with this book. If you've read anything that doesn't sit well with you, feel free to choose a way forward that you feel comfortable with. The whole purpose of the book is for you to create your own dream career and life, not mine, so it's important that you take on board the bits that resonate with you and feel confident enough to disregard anything that doesn't.

The same applies to advice you receive from other people.

The biggest tip I can give you in this area is that if someone is giving you advice about something, look carefully at how they are living their life, observe what their principles are, what they believe and what they are trying to achieve, and interpret their advice based on that analysis.

For example, I love my family and value their opinions, but none of them live a life that I would want, so why would I listen to any advice they have for me when it comes to career choice or lifestyle? Just because people are older than you doesn't necessarily mean that they know better. It often means that they come from a different era with different principles and different life goals. From a time when everyone accepted that work wasn't meant to be fun and you just had to put up with it in order to pay the bills.

That simply is not true anymore.

So, when looking for advice or guidance, seek out someone who already has the type of career you want or who is already living the type of life you desire, and listen to him or her.

It's unlikely that someone who doesn't believe in your dream is going to be able to advise you how to make it come true, although there is one slight caveat to this point.

Often, the best advice can come from people who never took the steps that you now want to take, but who deeply regret not doing so. There are many people approaching the end of their lives with limited time remaining who wish they had lived the life they wanted to live when they had the chance, just like you have the chance now. They would give anything to swap places with you because they know the regret of never trying is far worse than any fear you might experience which is holding you back. The problem with regret is that you don't know about it until it's too late.

I don't have enough time

Aside from all of the various things I've already talked about in this chapter, the single most common excuse I ever hear for people not doing something that they say they would otherwise do is that they don't have enough time, hence my desire to address it separately.

For the most part, it's the biggest load of nonsense ever.

Here's why.

Apart from in a very few extreme circumstances I've seen over the years, every single person who has used time as an excuse is either being egotistical or arrogant as discussed earlier, or they're just kidding themselves. Or both.

Are you reading this right now and being offended immediately because you *are* one of those people who just doesn't have the time to do whatever it is you keep saying you want to do? Chances are you're full of shit.

Do you watch TV? Do you use social media? How about WhatsApp? Do you go shopping, watch sports or waste any other time in your day?

If so you do have time, you're just choosing to spend it on other things.

At the time of writing, Apple has just released its new operating system that delivers a report about the time I spend on my phone every week. For the last seven days, I've spent an average of six hours and 36 minutes on my phone. Per day. In one week, I spent 14 hours 54 minutes on WhatsApp and three hours 43 minutes on Twitter.

Until I received that report I would never have guessed it was that much, and very little of that time can be justified as anything more than wasted. Granted, we all need a bit of down time, but the amount we all waste without realising is huge.

How much are you wasting?

The key is to ...

Audit your time

Whenever I feel as though I'm not getting things done that I want to complete, I start keeping a record of the time I'm spending on various tasks each day, from the moment I wake up to the moment I go to sleep.

By being completely ruthless with that analysis it becomes pretty easy to create time and space to complete key tasks.

You might be screaming at me now saying that it's just not possible for you to free up any time, but that's extremely unlikely to be true. In fact, if you were at a live event with me at which we could go through this process in person, I'd be happy to bet a crisp £50 note that I could find time in your diary that you don't think exists.

Let's use a few more dramatic examples that you might not have considered, over and above the standard *"watch less Netflix"* that you might expect from a book like this.

Exercise

Do you have kids that you love to use as your biggest excuse for everything? If so, how much of your time every day is spent on them? A lot, I'd guess.

Let's get creative. If you run your kids to school every day and that takes up an hour of your day, could you create a lift share with parents in your area to take turns doing the school run to free up time on a few days a week? Do you cook more than once per week? If so, how much time does that take up? Could you batch cook on a Sunday afternoon so that you have enough food for the week and free up an hour or more every evening?

Think of your own standard timetable. Rather than assuming everything you do is necessary and immovable, start from a basis of questioning everything from scratch and brainstorm ways that you could create an extra hour here or there. Even if you can create an extra two hours a week, that's 104 hours over the next year – or almost two full weeks of full working days that you could dedicate to changing your life. If you create five hours per week, that's 260 hours during the year – the equivalent of more than a month of standard working days.

This applies more than anything if you are fortunate enough to be in a position where you are cash rich but time poor. If that is the case, you have no excuses and just need to start trading more of your disposable cash for more time. Using the examples above, send your kids to school in an Uber and start using a service that delivers pre-prepared healthy meals to your door, and you'll instantly create more time than you need to transform your life.

Ultimately, if you really, really want to make the time, you will. You must also remember that we all have the same number of hours in a day and no one is going to hand you any extra, so you have to create your own by making sacrifices and/or being crafty.

Time is running out

If none of the preceding pages of this chapter have been enough to convince you to put your excuses to one side, I hope this last blow is enough to shock you into action.

What follows is one of the single most powerful illustrations I have ever seen. It comes from the *Wait But Why* blog of Tim Urban entitled 'Your Life In Weeks' which you can find in full using your favourite search engine.

In summary, it shows a chart of a life broken down into the number of weeks we have, assuming we live until we're 90 years old. Fifty two weeks across by 90 years down. When you take away the weeks from the end of your life that you're already putting to one side for retirement, then cross out all of the weeks you've already used up, you might realise that you don't have that many weeks left to do all of the things that you want to do.

Best not to waste anymore.

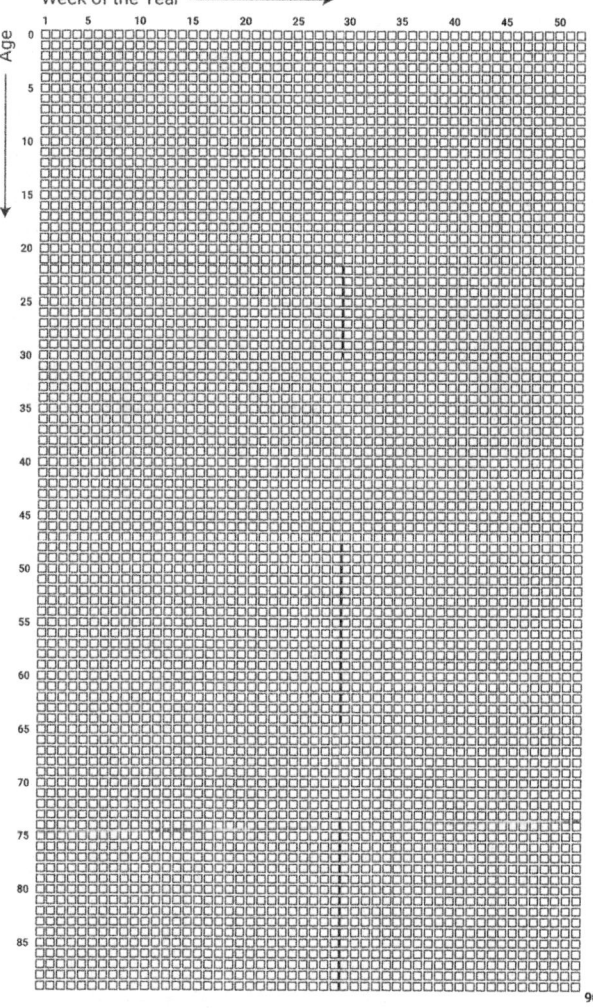

Here's my life with the weeks I've had up to age 38 blacked out, and the weeks from when I turned 70 greyed out. It leaves me with fewer than 1,600 weeks to do all of the things I want to do in my working life. The first 2,000 went in the blink of an eye.

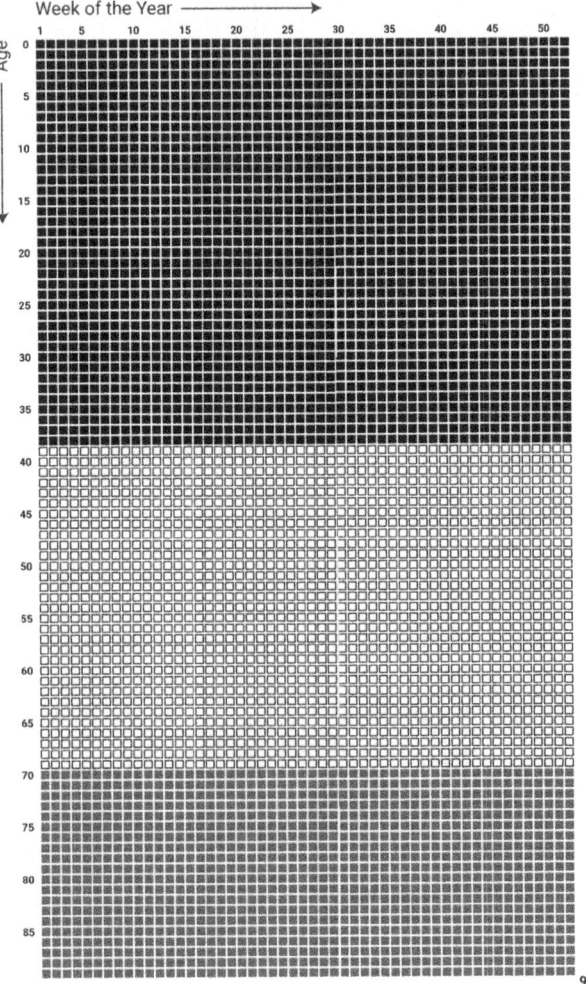

Limiting Beliefs

As discussed earlier, the things you believe prevent you from moving forward are often just the stories that you tell yourself that turn into limiting beliefs. You will tell yourself you're just the way you are as a way of justifying whatever it is that you're not doing.

Do you ever look at a friend and wish you were more like them for something?

Maybe they always know where to start, or always get things done, while you just procrastinate. Maybe they believe in themselves in a way that you don't.

Or maybe you just choose to focus on their strengths while focusing on your weaknessesw. Maybe when you don't do something you tell yourself the story that it's because you're too afraid to do it, but aren't there loads of other examples in your life of things you've done that you were once afraid of but did them anyway?

Haven't you achieved lots of things in your life that, when you started out, didn't seem possible? Maybe you tell yourself different stories about those times compared to the stories you tell yourself about things you believe you can't do.

I'd guess that whatever you do for a living now you had to learn about it at some point. At the very least, there was once a time in your life when you couldn't read, and now you're reading this, which is pretty impressive. I know we take for granted things like reading and walking once we can do them, but have you ever watched how long it takes a kid to learn this stuff? It's hard work, but they just keep going until they've cracked it because they never tell themselves that it can't be done and give up.

Maybe it's just time to focus on all of the things you've done in your life, on all of your strengths and the things that other people see as your skills. If you don't think you have any ask a few of your friends and family members what they would say you're good at. Or go back over your life and career to date and write down everything that you've done that once upon a time you couldn't do. Then focus on how you overcame whatever challenges lay in front of you when you wanted to achieve those goals. Apply the same level of belief to whatever it is that you want to do now, rather than telling yourself the story that you can't do it.

That story simply isn't true. You are capable of so much more than you ever thought possible.

Exercise

What was that, you want another exercise to do? No problem. For this one you just need a big piece of paper and a good marker pen.

Write *"All Of The Great Things I've Done"* in big letters at the top of the page. Next, list as many things as you can that you've achieved in your life, big or small, then write alongside each one a summary of how you did each one.

If you struggle to give yourself credit for anything, think of things that your most generous relative or friend would say was an achievement and use them instead.

The next page shows an example of how it should start off, and your target is to fill the page. Once it's finished, you should put it on a wall that you see every day, adding to it whenever you think of something else that you've done in the past or whenever you do something new that you should be proud of.

When you find yourself having any doubts about what you are capable of, you should simply read your list and remember how brilliant you are.

ALL OF THE GREAT THINGS I'VE DONE

GOT MY JOB
- 🔍 LOOKED FOR JOBS I MIGHT LIKE
- APPLIED FOR A FEW OF THEM
- READ UP ON SOME STUFF
- WENT FOR INTERVIEWS
- YES! GOT THE JOB!

TAUGHT MY DAUGHTER TO RIDE HER BIKE
- WATCHED SOME YOUTUBE TUTORIAL VIDEOS
- BOUGHT ALL OF THE EQUIPMENT
- STARTED SLOWLY
- HELPED HER TO PRACTISE FOR 2 MONTH UNTIL SHE COULD DO IT!

LEARNED HOW TO DRIVE
- GOT AN INSTRUCTOR
- BOOKED LESSONS
- PRACTISED WITH MY DAD
- KEPT GOING UNTIL I COULD DO IT!

SET UP A SWEET SHOP IN SCHOOL
- ASKED THE TEACHERS FOR PERMISSION
- BOUGHT SOME BOXES OF DAMAGED SWEETS FROM MY UNCLE TONY!
- FIGURED OUT HOW MUCH I NEEDED TO SELL THEM ALL
- SOLD THEM!

Bear in mind that it is likely that you are talking to yourself constantly throughout the day, and the way we talk to ourselves can tend to be far more negative than the way we talk to any of our friends or anyone who we are trying to encourage.

The follow up exercise to the one above, therefore, is to begin to notice how you are talking to yourself. Simply start observing the thoughts going through your mind throughout the day.

If you are finding yourself being negative, mean or nasty to yourself on a regular basis, or telling yourself all of the ways you can't do something that you might quite like to do, or beating yourself up unnecessarily, remember the things that you have written down on your big piece of paper and tell the mean little voice in your mind to be quiet so that the positive voice can have some time in the limelight for a change.

It can take time, but it is possible to slowly change the way your mind reacts to the outside world. The trick is to be conscious of whenever it is being mean and negative, and purposefully change it to being upbeat and positive. Over time, you should find that the positivity becomes your default setting, which makes everything else much more enjoyable.

The key is to bear in mind that this isn't the usual *"just think happy thoughts"* bullshit that I hear everywhere. It's not about deluding yourself that things are great if they're not. It is about noticing the ways in which you talk to yourself, being conscious of whether any negative thoughts are unreasonable and, if they are, making sure that you consciously tell your brain that there's no need to be so mean.

If, on the other hand, your brain is noticing something you're doing that isn't very nice, be aware of that and make a conscious effort to change your behaviour in the future so that you don't have to beat yourself up about it anymore.

If you are able to work through everything in this chapter and rid your life of the various challenges and inhibitions we've discussed, you'll practically be bullet proof and ready to storm into the next secret, which I absolutely love and which is, you'll be pleased to hear, a lot lighter, brighter and more fun than lots of the darkness we've just covered.

"I close my eyes and I can see,
the world that's waiting up for me
That I call my own
Through the dark, through the door,
through where no one's been before
But it feels like home
They can say, they can say it all sounds crazy.
They can say, they can say I've lost my mind
I don't care, I don't care, so call me crazy,
we can live in a world that we design

Every night I lie in bed,
the brightest colours fill my head
A million dreams are keeping me awake
I think of what the world could be,
a vision of the one I see
A million dreams is all it's gonna take
A million dreams for the world
we're gonna make"

−A MILLION DREAMS,
THE GREATEST SHOWMAN

7

SECRET 5
ECSTASY

Enough of the serious stuff.

If the last chapter was my favourite child, then this chapter is my favourite dog.

This is my little white, gorgeous, scruffy, fun-filled puppy bouncing into my bedroom every morning, jumping up onto the bed and licking me all over my face while screaming:

"IT'S ANOTHER DAY, DAD! CAN YOU BELIEVE IT, IT'S ANOTHER DAY AND WE ONLY JUST HAD ONE YESTERDAY! THIS IS INCREDIBLE! ISN'T IT? ISN'T IT INCREDIBLE? OH MY GOD IMAGINE WHAT WE CAN DO TODAY! WE CAN GO ON ANOTHER WALK, CAN'T WE DAD? CAN'T WE? WILL THAT CAT BE THERE AGAIN? OH, I HOPE THAT CAT'S THERE AGAIN, I'LL CATCH HER TODAY, DAD. I'LL DEFINITELY CATCH HER TODAY. OH MY GOD THIS IS THE BEST DAY OF MY ENTIRE LIFE!"

Every day. No exception. Every day that's what she's like. Never bored, never tired of going on a walk, never fed up unless, of course, I won't play, in which case she just sits in the corner and sulks with her big brown eyes peering up at me while her head rests on the floor. She's got it down to a tee. As soon as I pick up her lead, she does that thing that only dogs can do, where they jump up and spin around 360 degrees in one go as an outward display to the world of how happy they are.

And that's the point of this entire book. The exercises that have gone before, the maths and the fear analysis. The heavy-duty stuff and recalling misery in our minds.

Here's where all of the hard work leads.

There's no point going through the challenges of stripping away all of the things that are currently making you miserable without having something extraordinary to aim for. If you want to change your career and, ultimately, your life, you need to have a target that will drag you kicking and screaming towards it, even on those days when you just want to sit on your couch eating chocolate and watching Netflix. (As an aside, that's what I thought Netflix and chill meant until I discovered otherwise one day and realised it wasn't a pastime I should be broadcasting in public …)

So, here's what I want you to do next.

Exercise

Take five minutes to sit quietly by yourself. Get away from your work colleagues, your other half, your kids, your dog, the cat next door, and turn off the TV. Read these instructions very carefully, then close your eyes and drift away. It is very important that you read the instructions before you close your eyes, not the other way around, otherwise the system doesn't work. It's also extremely important that you don't drift away if you're listening to this while driving or operating heavy machinery ...

I want you to take yourself back to the first time you realised that the world wasn't everything you thought it could be. It might be the first time an adult told you that dreams were for children and you needed to grow up and act your age, or it might be the first time you watched something on the news that told you that our planet is a horrible and frightening place to be feared.

Go back to that day in your mind, then think of everything that happened to you before that day. Let yourself float away to a place before a reality created by other people destroyed your hopes and dreams and convinced you an average, grey, mundane life was all you could wish for because that's what everybody else has.

What did you dream of being? Who did you think you would be? Deep inside your soul, when you allow yourself to connect with the little person you once were, what do you see, what do you hear and what do you feel?

Think of any little kids you have in your family. They might be your own children, your grandkids or your nieces, nephews or cousins. If you don't have any in your family think of the last time you walked past a kid in the street or in the supermarket; think about that look of wonder in their eyes. What are they dreaming of doing or being when they grow up, knowing they can do whatever they want?

I was walking in the woods with my puppy and my wife a few months ago. It had been raining heavily for days and the rain had subsided enough to make a lovely crisp, sunny day for walking while leaving plenty of mud and puddles along the forest pathways. We approached a family of a mum, dad and two little boys around four and six years old. The boys had dark, ruffled hair and were dressed in red rain macs, water proof trousers and wellington boots.

From a distance I could see that both of the little men were absolutely soaked and covered from head to toe in mud. It was dripping from their ears and running down their noses. As I turned to my wife to ask why she thought they were so wet considering it hadn't been raining all day, the eldest of the boys took a running jump from a kerb at the side of the path into a muddy puddle of water a metre wide. As he landed in the middle of the expanse of water the splash soaked him, his little brother and his mum in one fell swoop.

They all burst out laughing, and my wife and I giggled as we noticed the dad was staying well away from the chaos to avoid getting filthy himself.

It was so lovely and heart-warming to watch.

Do you remember that amount of joy from something so simple? Do you remember pretending to be something incredible and feeling joy ripple through your body, before anyone told you it wasn't possible?

That's what I want you to remember. Whatever it was when you were growing up that made you happy. The thread that ran through your life that you might have lost along the way.

Just focus on it now. Picture it in your mind and look at the scene through your own eyes. What were the colours like? Were there any smells or any sounds? Make them brighter, stronger and louder. Double the intensity, then double it again. Feel the vibrations of that memory flood through your veins and fill your heart with calm, peace and happiness.

When I think back to the days before the world started to corrupt my soul there was a combination of things that I loved. As you already know I was always an artist and an entrepreneur and, although nobody spotted the latter, it was always clear that the former was in my blood. There's an artistic streak that runs through both sides of my family, with my granddad on my mum's side a gifted poet and my grandad on my dad's side a keen amateur painter who loved to create works of art throughout his retirement. That thread passed through a few of my cousins and me, and showed itself through pencil drawings, paintings and other creative ventures, all of which were embraced when we were children but slowly ebbed away as the 'real' world told us those things are for kids.

I was told when applying to do a law degree at university that they wouldn't accept art as a relevant A-Level, which meant I dropped it after I turned 16 to do an extra maths qualification because, as we all know, you can't have enough trigonometry and Pythagoras knowledge in the real world.

It gives me great pleasure when speaking to anyone who supports traditional education models to confirm that I have not once in my adult life outside of school ever used any of my advanced maths knowledge that was apparently so vital to preparing for a law degree.

Unfortunately, that theme was only ever going to continue once I'd joined the world of corporate law. It won't surprise you to hear that creative talents aren't exactly encouraged and developed in that world either.

So, for years and years, I buried my artistic side without even realising it. It's clearly forced its way out in dramatic ways through the creation of companies and wild dreams, allowing me to design logos and websites to at least satisfy some of my artistic urges (my subconscious finding ways to meet my otherwise unmet needs).

But it was only last week that I was in an art shop to buy some picture frames for my newly purchased inspirational Mohamed Ali photographs when I just happened to walk down the aisle filled with sketchbooks and art pencils. Before I knew it, I'd picked up some supplies and was striding through the store with a smile on my face and a warmth inside that I hadn't felt since I was drawing those Teenage Mutant Hero Turtles when I was eight years old.

The other bit about that part of my life that I haven't told you though, is that despite being a clever kid and doing well in class, I had lots of friends and never felt different to anyone. In fact, as I alluded to earlier, whenever a new kid joined our class the teacher would sit them next to me because they knew I would look after them and help them to settle in before they found their own way and made their own friends.

I also always felt like I could see a different world to everyone else. I remember being four years old and wondering why adults couldn't see things that I could see. Not seeing dead people or anything Hollywood like that, but more that I often had a different perspective on life, even as a little boy and, as I grew, I could feel that I had an instinct for things that I couldn't explain.

So now I try to help other people and I've reconnected with my artistic side. I'm writing books, drawing and painting, and I'm making sure that I take time to rest, relax, laugh and jump in muddy puddles with my puppy.

What's your story? If I met you in the street and asked you to tell me about your childhood and whatever it was that lit you up and made you feel at peace with the world, what would you tell me?

Take as much time as you need now to write it all down on a big, blank piece of paper. Just start reminiscing and get as much down as possible. Keep writing as much as you can, all the time being aware of how you feel as you write each memory. If you can, write it with a pen or pencil on paper. I don't know what it is, but there's something therapeutic about doing it that way that just doesn't seem the same when typing on a computer. If you used to be or are still artistic, draw pictures of what you can remember and allow your creativity to explode onto the page.

Are there any of those stories and memories that continue a thread into your adult life? If any bad memories come to mind, consider what positives came from those incidents. Even in the worst of situations there should be some glimmer of positivity. Some of the greatest artists and musicians in history began their journeys through troubled childhoods that forced them to protect their siblings or retreat to the safety of their bedrooms with their guitar, with paper and pen in hand to write classic songs.

When you've got as much as you can down on paper, take a few minutes to think about how each memory makes you feel and to consider whether there are any patterns that resonate with you even now.

I realised through all of this that my purpose in this world is to help others while being true to my creative self. I've always believed in the impossible and when I was younger everyone believed in it with me. It's easy to tell an eight-year old that he can be whatever he wants in life. It's much harder for those same people to agree when a 35 year old who has been through the mill a few times keeps telling those around him that the impossible is possible.

I'm not here to tell you that you can do anything you ever wanted to do, though. I'm 38 years old and the chances of me ever playing professional football for Liverpool Football Club are diminishing by the day (although I'd be lying if I said I'd totally given up on the idea).

But I am here to tell you that if you dreamed of being a dancer when you were a kid and haven't danced properly for decades that you can start again now. You can follow the steps in this book and create the time and space in your life to start dancing again, to join a dance club and rekindle that fire in your belly that you thought was extinguished long ago.

If once upon a time you lost yourself painting pictures, building train sets or creating cartoons, it's time to roll back the years. The little boy or little girl inside you is waiting for you to come back.

Your dreams never died, they were just stored in the wishing machine in the centre of your soul, waiting for the day when they would come true. Waiting for the child who dreamed of a wonderful life to wake up again one day, to see the world for what it is and to reclaim their destiny.

It's time.

The trick at this stage is to figure out whether you can earn enough from whatever you love to turn it into a sustainable income, or whether you can find a job that satisfies all of the things that light you up.

Now, it's important to be careful here. This is the part of the story where lots of people will tell you to follow your passion, but I'm not going to do that for one very good reason.

Falafel.

"What has falafel got to do with anything?", you might ask, and you'd be right to do so.

Well, one of my best mates in the world, who's also a lawyer and has dreamed in the past of doing various other things, told me a while ago that he was going to open a falafel shop. He's originally from Sheffield and had lived in London for a decade, so he was keen to know whether falafel shops had found their way to the north of England.

Between you and me, I think he fancied himself as the Steve Jobs of falafel, the only problem being that he didn't invent them and had no way of monetising them other than to open a sandwich shop to sell them from, which created another problem that I spotted fairly early on.

You see, my mate doesn't particularly like getting up early.

I pointed out to him, as nicely as possible given that I'm not one for shattering dreams, that sandwich shops tend to have two busy times when they make most of their money, the first of which would mean he'd have to be at work for 5am every day to prepare for the morning rush.

It wasn't something he'd considered.

It turns out, as I've found out myself in years gone by, that sometimes we love to do something (or eat something) as a hobby, but often those things are best left as hobbies (or sandwiches).

Similarly, I love to cook and people have asked me in the past why I wouldn't train to be a chef. The simple answer is I would hate the hours and don't want to be stuck in a kitchen for long periods every day.

So, it's important to add a second part to creating a dream life, which is to think about all of the ways you would like your life to be structured to make it happy and fulfilling given your non-negotiable circumstances.

For example, if you have kids and one of your priorities is to spend as much time with them as possible, it's important that you design the next phase of your life to maximise that aspect.

Which takes us to the next exercise. You've had a long enough break since the last one, surely?

Exercise

Go back to the plan that you created as part of Chapter 4 – Secret 2. As a reminder, it looks like this but should be full of information on your version:

Current Number _____	The 7 Secrets to Change Your Career *www.changeyourcareer.org/essence*		Target Number _____
Everything you dislike, hate or despise about your current job and/or life:	What specifically is it that you don't like about it:	Why, why, why, why, why?	(We'll fill this column later)
1.			
2.			
3.			
4.			

Current Number ____	The 7 Secrets to Change Your Career *www.changeyourcareer.org/essence*		Target Number ____
Everything you dislike, hate or despise about your current job and/or life:	What specifically is it that you don't like about it:	Why, why, why, why, why?	(We'll fill this column later)
5.			
6.			
7.			
8.			
9.			
10.			

You'll remember in that table you identified all of the things that you dislike or hate about your current job and/or life, what specifically it is you don't like and what the root of the issues are.

So, what?

It's time to go back through your list from Chapter 4 and highlight the issues you still think are important to you after having been through the *"why?"* process and having had some time to reflect.

Next, whatever you're left with, go through each challenge and ask yourself the all-encompassing question, *"so, what?"*.

Let me explain.

Having learnt so much over the past 15 years, I think that everything I have discovered could well be boiled down to the *"so, what?"* principle. It doesn't work when you're in a heightened, stress-fuelled state and filled with rage, because at that point asking *"so, what?"* is likely to do nothing more than cause you to completely fly off the handle and go into Incredible Hulk mode.

But when you're in a calm and relaxed state, as you are now, going through each thing in your life that you've identified as being a big deal and asking yourself *"so, what?"* about it can be really cathartic.

For example, I used to get my knickers in a twist about the toilet lid being left up. Not the seat, but the lid that goes on top of the seat and covers the entire toilet bum-hole.

I think it started when I was working for a big law firm in London when I was 22 and the girls used to complain that some of the lads left the toilet seat up after using a shared toilet. Another male colleague and I pointed out politely that the girls don't have a God-given right for the toilet to be left in the ideal setting for them to use when they walk into the bathroom any more than the lads do, so the fairest way to leave the toilet was for the entire lid to be closed, meaning that both boys and girls had to lift up their relevant parts in order to use the system before returning it to its original, fully closed position.

I also just like some things to be left neat and tidy, and toilet lids being left up makes toilets look less tidy than they need to be. It became one of a number of real issues in my house, and was a small contributing factor to me being unhappy at home. I know, I know, I was a crank.

Now, though, if I see a toilet lid left up I just ask myself *"so, what?"* and all of a sudden it doesn't seem that important anymore. To expand on the question, I could say *"are you that bothered about this thing that you're prepared to get divorced over it?"* to which I can reply happily now to say … yes, absolutely I am.

Just kidding, the real answer is no, I'm not.

It's key that you go through each of your dislikes and do the same thing. If you were in a happy and fulfilled state already, would you be that bothered by the thing you've identified?

Once you've done that, cross out anything on your list that isn't a real problem in hindsight and you should be left with a list of the really important issues for you to address.

Now for the most important part.

Positive Target Setting

It's no good just having a list of things that you dislike about your job or your life. This is one of the biggest mistakes anyone makes when trying to make significant changes to anything: they focus on what they don't want, rather than what they do want.

It's the reason why telling kids not to jump in puddles doesn't work, and the basis for why when I say don't think of a zebra you can't help but think of a zebra.

Our brains might be capable of lots of things that completely mess us up, but they're not great at understanding negative commands, which is why "don't think of a zebra" leads you to think of a zebra before being able to reverse the process. It's also why kids will continue to jump in puddles – because their brains can only hear the positive part of the command, which means when you say *"don't jump in the puddles"* they hear *"don't JUMP IN THE PUDDLES"*, and they jump in the puddles, leading you to shout something like *"how many times do I need to tell you not to JUMP IN THE PUDDLES before you stop doing it?"*.

You see the problem?

Whether you want kids to stop kids jumping in puddles, you want to give up smoking or change your life, you need to think of the positive command that will replace the negative one. With smoking, you could use *"I want to be fit and healthy"* rather than *"I want to stop smoking"*, because fit and healthy people don't smoke.

For the purposes of this book, we need you to create a list of all of the ways you can stop doing the things you hate from your current position by replacing them with something positive.

Using the example from Chapter 4, if I discovered it was a key issue to avoid getting up early, I would list a positive goal of wanting to control my hours of work so I decide what time I get up.

Does that make sense?

Take as much time as you need to do that now and get in touch using my email address at the end of the book if you get stuck and need help.

As a hint for any practical things like hating having to share a toaster with people in your house because you all like to have it on different settings, I've realised recently that problems like that can be solved by having more than one toaster, or toasters with different sections for different settings.

It might seem daft, but if every day of your life starts with you being a little bit annoyed about your toast burning and you can solve it by spending £30 on another toaster, it seems more insane to carry on with your current system just because we all assume every house should only have one toaster because that's the way we were brought up.

Current Number _____	The 7 Secrets to Change Your Career www.changeyourcareer.org/essence		Target Number _____
Everything you dislike, hate or despise about your current job and/or life:	What specifically is it that you don't like about it:	Why, why, why, why, why?	What positive target can you set that will change this aspect of your life?
1.			
2.			
3.			
4.			
5.			

Current Number ____	The 7 Secrets to Change Your Career *www.changeyourcareer.org/essence*		Target Number ____
Everything you dislike, hate or despise about your current job and/or life:	What specifically is it that you don't like about it:	Why, why, why, why, why?	What positive target can you set that will change this aspect of your life?
6.			
7.			
8.			
9.			
10.			

After you've completed all of that, it's time to go onto the final planning step.

"It's funny how your dreams change as you're growing old You don't wanna be no spaceman, you just want the gold All the dream stealers are lying in wait But if you wanna be a spaceman, it's still not too late"

—D'YER WANNA BE A SPACEMAN, OASIS

Choosing Your Next Venture

I'm conscious I've thrown this bit in without much of a fanfare, so hopefully it's crept up on you without you freaking out.

There is a method in my madness.

While my childhood of being certain of what I wanted to be when I grew up went a bit haywire in my teenage years, and again later in life, something it gave me for which I am grateful is complete immunity from most children's torture of being asked perpetually what they wanted to do with their lives and having no idea what that one thing was.

It annoys me that this was ever a topic of conversation and, for some people, still is. It is nothing short of ludicrous that anyone should make a decision about their career that they are expected to stick to for the rest of their lives, especially in this day and age, and especially children or young adults.

Have you ever felt overwhelmed by the idea of choosing a career? Or do you ever avoid changing from something you dislike or even hate because you wouldn't know what to do next anyway? Do you worry about committing to a new job in case you make the wrong decision?

They seem to be the issues most people face when trying to decide what to do next with their lives. So, before we get into how to pick what's next, it's important to address a bigger point.

Whatever you choose to do next does not need to be for the rest of your life. It does not need to be for the next 10 years and you don't need to be 100 per cent certain, beyond any shadow of a doubt, that it will be everything you always dreamed of.

By making what you do next into something bigger than it needs to be, you are creating problems that don't exist that could prevent you from getting to where you want to be. Instead, allow yourself to believe in a new reality that you might never have been told about before and might be completely contrary to everything you have ever been taught in the past.

The reality, if you choose to believe it, is that your options in the modern world are endless and it is no longer necessary to choose one thing to do for the rest of your life.

I understand that this might seem like another red or blue pill moment from *The Matrix*; a choice between a world you've always believed to be real and some other world that you've heard about but never thought really existed.

But it does exist. I live there and so do millions of others. It's a place where what you do to pay your bills isn't necessarily what you do for eight to 12 hours per day. A world where, if you choose to, you can create a stable income doing one thing while spending the rest of your time exploring what else to do with your life to bring you true joy and happiness. A world where you can free yourself from the shackles of what everyone told you was real and, instead, inhabit a place where the rules as you've always known them no longer apply.

I appreciate this might sound crazy, but hopefully by now we've broken down enough barriers for me to start talking like a crazy person and for you not to dismiss what I'm saying out of hand.

By the time you've read through the next few paragraphs you might actually be annoyed, even angry, that you've been stuck in whatever you've been doing so far in your life when this other world existed all along. I hope you are upset, because that will give you all of the motivation you need to go through with the decisions that you need to make to charge forward into your new life.

It all goes back to something I mentioned in passing earlier. Whatever you do now to earn money to pay for the rest of your life, that income can be replaced in a heartbeat in ways you might not have contemplated before. I have witnessed people switch from being car mechanics to social media marketers and replace their previous full-time salary within a month by taking on six local businesses as clients. I have seen first-hand people who you might class as perfectly normal transform from being stuck in full time, miserable employment to travelling the world telling their stories as public speakers.

The options are endless once you choose to go down the rabbit hole and start exploring. And while this book isn't designed to choose for you what you should do next, I will show you how to make that decision and provide resources to inspire you.

In my view there are two ways you can decide what to do next that will give you the life that you've always dreamed of. You can either:

1   pick something that you've always wanted to do or that jumps out at you as a dream job having been through the exercises we've done so far (because not trying to do that thing will mean you always wonder what it would have been like); or

2   use all of the factors that you've identified as being key to you living a happy life and reverse engineer what that should be.

Taking each one in turn …

If You Already Know

In my experience it's unlikely this will apply to you if you've spent a long time in a job or career that you don't like. If it does apply to you, and you have just never had the courage or the motivation to move forward with your dream career, the exercises you've been through in this book should hopefully help you to overcome whatever has been holding you back.

If you still feel stuck, please contact me at the email address at the end of the book setting out whatever you're stuck on and I'll do everything I can to help.

If you are ready to get started, but don't know where to begin, there's a list of resources at www.changeyourcareer.org/resources that should help you to get going. Failing that I'd recommend typing *"how to do X"* into Google and start from there.

It really is that simple.

Reverse Engineering

I always think saying that I reverse engineered a business sounds great. I've got no idea why, but whenever I describe to people how I created my online business, when I get to say *"reverse engineered"* I feel like some kind of business guru. Maybe it's because I think engineers are cool and create real things from nothing, or maybe it's just because the phrase sounds impressive in itself.

Either way, that's the next step.

The big goal is to take each of the smaller goals you've created in the previous part, write them down next to each other in the simplest terms possible, then start thinking about what jobs or businesses you could do that would tick all of the boxes of your dream life. If you can't tick them all, it's about thinking of things that will tick as many as possible, beginning with the most important.

A key thing to say here is that if you can reverse engineer the constituent parts of your dream life back to something that you absolutely love to do, that is dream target level 10. That's Jedi mind tricks and flying super-heroes all rolled into one. If you can do that you've absolutely nailed it.

But that's not essential.

My most recent version of this exercise led to me doing what I do now, which is something I really enjoy and pays me enough money to live a happy life. I also have enough free time to pursue other things that I love.

It's not playing football for a living or being a rock star, but it enables me to play football in my spare time if I want to, and to learn how to play the guitar.

That could, ultimately, mean that I can set myself another goal for some future point in time whereby, for example, I might be able to earn money playing the guitar, or being a football coach or analyst.

At this moment in time, though, it doesn't have to be all things to all men or all women.

It's imperative to remember throughout this process that we shouldn't overestimate what we can do in a week but underestimate what we can do in a year, or in two or five years.

If I offered you a guarantee that in two years you would be free of your current miserable job and transformed into something more fulfilling and exciting, with the opportunity for it to become even more fulfilling and exciting in the future, would you bite my hand off?

To expand further on my decisions when I restructured my life leading to where I am now, I decided that I wanted a role that allowed me to control my own time and gave me a steady, reliable, recurring monthly income doing work that I enjoyed – helping people to improve their lives and their businesses. The goal was to do that for no more than 30 per cent of my week so that I had the other 70 per cent to focus on what I describe as my 'moon shot' projects, one of which you are currently reading.

That structure allows me to have a stable home life that depends solely on me and my time without any external risks or employees to deal with, while giving me the flexibility and freedom to take shots at the moon with other projects, without any risk that the failure of those projects will jeopardise the stability of my home life.

The issue with my previous ventures was that everything was tied up in the same pot. If the businesses took off I could make lots of money which, back then, I mistakenly thought was the path to happiness and fulfilment, but they also were inextricably linked to my personal income, which meant that when, for example, my online business started to hit the rocks, not only was my dream shattered but my personal financial position was in ruins.

With my new structure I don't have any of those problems, and I can decide whether or not to take on new one-to-one clients depending on how much money I decide that I'd like to earn in any particular period.

And this is where the counting exercise in Chapter 5 comes into play.

One of the biggest perceived fears I see in people that stops them moving from a job that makes them miserable is the idea that they can't afford to move. They focus on the big, impressive salary number that they're paid as an employee, or the gross figure that they take from their company if they're self-employed, without considering that isn't what they actually have as a disposable income every month or what they need to survive.

By having the latter numbers identified, it helps to focus the mind on exactly how much you need each month to be able to survive, which is usually much more manageable than the big, gross salary number that we tend to get hung up on.

Let's say, hypothetically, that you need £3,000 every month to be able to pay your mortgage or rent, all essential utility bills and non-negotiable outgoings. If you are thinking of starting a consultancy business helping people with whatever you currently do now, you don't need to replace your current gross salary, you only need £3,000 per month (or six clients paying you £500 each) and you'd have your basic needs covered. Seeing as you'd need to account a bit more for tax and general business expenses, let's call it seven clients at £500 each per month.

Then all you need to do is ask whether you back yourself to get seven clients. If the answer to that is that you don't, I'd firstly say that you are 100 per cent wrong and, secondly, ask do you back yourself to get one client or to sell one thing to one customer?

I do. I back you to be able to do it. With everything you've already achieved in life and all of the skills and experience you've gained, you would have no issues in getting one client or customer on board. You just need to believe in yourself and remember that there are plenty of people out there with far less skill and experience than you who are already doing what you think you can't do.

So, can we agree that you could get one client, or one customer if I put a gun to your head and you had no other option?

Great, because if you can get one client or customer, you just need to repeat the same process six more times and you've got yourself covered. After that, it's just a question of how many clients or customers you want and how much money you want to earn compared to how much free time you want, which will all depend on your personal goals.

This is how I break down every complex task I ever come across, and I'd recommend highly that you do the same. I call it my *"can I tile a bathroom"* theory. Granted, it's not the snappiest title in the world, but it is what it is.

Let me take you back to 2008.

*   *   *

I'm working in one of the biggest corporate law firms in the world having qualified two years earlier. I'm working long hours and earning good money, but I'm keen to push on and do more. I've been dating my girlfriend for three years and we're pretty confident that we'll be together for a while, so we decide having seen others do it that we're going to do a property development together.

I decide to approach it in a different way to most people. I drive around the area in which we want to buy making a note of all of the run-down properties, then search the Land Registry in England to see who owns them. I write to each one offering to buy their house without the need for them to incur estate agent's fees.

I get a few replies, including one from a guy who loves the different approach. He agrees to sell to us for a price we're really happy with, and we set about renovating it from the absolute mess it's in, to something fit for students or young professionals to rent. I do a quick estimate and think that we can renovate the entire property for under £15,000, which my girlfriend's dad's boss (who's a builder) thinks is naively low, but we get to work anyway.

We're getting most quotes to come in on or under budget, except for the bathroom. After seeing a few plumbers and tilers and getting quotes that would take us well over our budget, I decide one day I'll do it myself.

"Since when have you been a tiler?" my girlfriend says.

"I'm not one, but it can't be that difficult surely?"

"It might not be difficult for a tiler, but I think there's a bit of a difference between that and a junior lawyer having a go at it!"

"Look at it this way. Do you believe that I can take one tile, put tile adhesive on the back, stick it to the wall so that it doesn't fall off and make sure it's straight?"

"Er, well, yeah, I suppose so"

"Great, so I just need to do that 200 times and I'll have tiled a whole room."

*   *   *

And that's what happened. I tiled a whole room, then knocked down and built an internal partition wall using the same theory before fitting a kitchen in the next development and, ultimately, fitting two bathrooms in our own city centre apartment a few years later complete with fancy boxes and spotlights that I'd fitted for extra impact.

The point is, whatever challenge you're facing, rather than building it up to being some great, big problem floating above your head like a storm cloud, break it down into its constituent parts and ask yourself whether you can complete that small task. If you can do it once, you can do it 10 times, or 100 times or, eventually if you really want to, a million times.

Once you've broken down everything that you'd like to do into its smaller parts, the trick is to write each of those parts down and brainstorm ideas about what careers would tick the boxes that you need to be ticked.

I've already mentioned what my requirements for my most recent business were, and I went through the same process before building my online gambling business in 2014.

The constituent parts of that were:

- something online that I could work on from anywhere with no fixed hours
- infinitely scalable with a small team of employees
- the ability to outsource as much as possible to third party contractors
- recession-proof
- something fun
- something I was interested in that I would enjoy working on.

When I brainstormed potential businesses that ticked those boxes, I came up with an online gambling company. I knew that I wouldn't be able to compete with the huge businesses already dominating that space, so came up with an idea in a niche area of the market that nobody else was targeting at that time. And, voila, a new business was born.

Now, as time wore on, I realised there were downsides to that business concept that I hadn't accounted for which I've alluded to already, namely that if I was running that business as my main company my entire life was resting on a moon shot being a success. That led to an unnecessarily high level of stress associated with it and decisions being made that I might not have made had I enjoyed more personal financial stability.

So, having been through that experience, when I went through the process again I took into account all of the mistakes I'd made and developed the next phase of my life so that I have a small consultancy business that provides my bread and butter income and which covers all of my essential outgoings each month, while having time, space and energy to write a book, develop other business ideas and bring back my online game without any financial pressure. What that means is that I have completely de-risked my life from a financial perspective. I don't rely on big projects to make money, and everything is far more secure and stable than it ever was before.

And that's how you go from having a fixed income determined by someone else outside of your control, to earning as much money as you want to earn while balancing the rest of your life around it to suit your personal needs and the needs of anyone around you.

Although, starting your own business isn't the only option for you at this stage.

Other Options

I have a natural tendency towards starting businesses in order to solve the problem of working in a miserable job and living a miserable life because that's what I did to escape. But that isn't the only way forward for you, so don't be afraid if you've been screaming at the pages of this book that you don't want to start your own company.

There are a number of other options you could consider based on the analysis you have carried out and what your desires are for the next phase of your career and life.

You could:

- reduce your hours in your current role, freeing up more time to do things that you want to do while maintaining a fixed income to cover your non-negotiable outgoings. If you've identified that you could survive on a portion of your current salary, or you can think of ways that you could, for example, work from home in order to be more productive, save travel time and, therefore, create more time to work on side projects, you could negotiate with your current employer to restructure what you currently do in order to make it work better for you[2];

- change your role within the company you work for to do something that ticks more of the boxes of things you enjoy doing;

- carry on doing the same job you do now but move to another company more closely aligned with your values, allowing you more flexibility with your time or to work from home;

---

[2]   For more detailed advice on how to negotiate doing this with your boss, check out Step IV – L is for Liberation in *The 4-Hour Work Week* by Tim Ferriss.

- change jobs to do something in another industry that appeals to your desires;

- become a consultant, or move to an organisation within your current industry that pays a portion of the income you earn or will pay you for the work you do, allowing you complete control over your time and salary (see, for example, Excello Law for lawyers in the UK, which changes the traditional model of employing lawyers and gives you a cut of everything you earn); or

- take a break (see more on this later).

Exercise

This exercise is effectively the culmination of everything we've been working towards.

Again, it's one for a big piece of paper and a marker pen. Write at the top in big letters "What I Want To Do Next", then down the left hand side write all of the answers you wrote in the table earlier in this chapter setting out the positive targets you can set that would overcome the bits you dislike or hate about your current career.

Next, add in anything you love to do or that lights you up when you think about it that, in an ideal world, you would do for a living.

Finally, start brainstorming on the rest of the page the things you could do that might achieve your positive targets while, if possible, also hitting your dream level 10 status. Once you've got a full list of ideas, you can start assessing each of them to see which one or more fits best.

To give you an idea of what to do, this is what my one looked like before I made my last transition to where I am now:

WHAT DO I WANT TO DO NEXT?

POSITIVE TARGETS

 CONTROL MY HOURS OF WORK

 BE MY OWN BOSS

 WORK FROM ANYWHERE

 GET PAID FOR WHAT I ACTUALLY DO

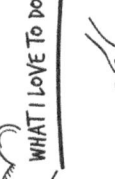 FEEL FULFILLED

WHAT I LOVE TO DO

 HELP OTHER PEOPLE

 WRITE / DRAW / BE CREATIVE

 SOLVE PROBLEMS

INTERACT WITH PEOPLE AND HAVE FUN

IDEAS

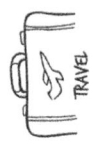   WRITE A BOOK

BE A CONSULTANT

 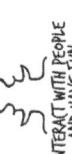 VOLUNTEER FOR A CHARITY

TRAVEL

 START A PODCAST OR YOUTUBE CHANNEL

Taking a Break

I think this mini-topic deserves a section to itself, regardless of what you've come up with in the last exercise.

I know how it feels to be in a place where, even with the best of intentions, your brain is just so frazzled and you've been doing the same thing for so long that you can no longer see the wood for the trees.

If that's you, it might be worth considering taking a complete break from everything for six to 12 months while you figure out exactly what it is that you want to do next.

I know, I know, your immediate reaction to that suggestion might be complete and utter incredulity. But bear with me.

If you feel like you have no idea which way to turn, even after going through all of the exercises in this book, you've probably been on the hamster wheel for so long that you have no idea which way is up. If that's the case, creating the time and space for a proper break could be the best decision you ever make, allowing yourself to consider exactly what you want to do with your life before making any decisions.

While previously it might have sounded impossible for you to even consider such a wild idea, hopefully having been through a few of the exercises in this book you'll see that it's not so crazy after all.

Let's say that you're willing to entertain the idea but a load of fears and excuses immediately spring to mind as to why you couldn't possibly do it in practice. Just go through the exercises in the previous chapters again to figure out what specifically would be stopping you and focus on all of the ways that you could overcome those challenges.

Remember, if you tell yourself you can't do it then the universe will confirm absolutely that you can't, but if you ask yourself how could you do it, you'll get as many answers as you can handle setting out all the ways in which it's possible.

You don't think you can afford it? Use the essential outgoings calculation to see how much you'd need to put aside to take one, two, three or six months off and brainstorm all of the ways in which you could put that money aside or earn it doing something other than your current job.

You worry about not being able to come back to your job after a break? Run the idea past your boss as a thought exercise and see how they react. For all you know, they might be happy to take your wage off the payroll temporarily and guarantee that your position would be safe to return to after a sabbatical.

If you feel completely burnt out to the level that you just don't know what to do next, I'd say that considering this as a real option is at the very least worth exploring.

Patience

Whatever you decide to do next, always remember that the most valuable tool in your armoury is patience. Whenever we want to change anything in our lives we tend to be sold quick fixes that appeal to our inherent lazy streaks, but the harsh reality is that the greatest achievements come only when we commit to hard work and dedication to a cause.

If you set your expectations that everything will transform in your career and life from misery to bliss in a matter of weeks, you are as likely to fail as you are if you try to get that six-pack four weeks before your summer holiday after 30 years of beer and pizzas have given you a portly appearance.

Alternatively, if you set yourself a realistic target based on patience and a step by step transformation in the same way that you might train for a marathon, you will be amazed at how quickly you will be able to change everything.

Don't overestimate what you can do in a month but underestimate what you can do in a year, and remember that you might need one or more stepping stones to get to where you ultimately want to end up. You might want to be a dance teacher and need two years to train, so for those two years you can restructure your life to allow yourself the time to re-train while still earning enough to cover your essential outgoings.

Whatever you might have been convinced of by normal society, ignore it. Just because you might be over 30 years old it doesn't mean you're past it and have no time left. If you need any inspiration for what can be achieved later in life, look up the stories of Colonel Sanders, who finally got his chicken recipe to the public with KFC at the age of 62, Ray Kroc of McDonald's fame, who found success at 52, or Charles Flint, who launched IBM at 61.

Be like the Chinese bamboo tree. Lay your foundations, build your base patiently without the need for external approval or validation then, when the time is right, you'll be ready to grow faster than you ever thought possible. But, importantly, don't expect everything to be a bed of roses along the way. Nothing worth doing in life is easy, so expect to come across some challenges and embrace them as part of the adventure. Think of it like when you start going to the gym again after months or years away. Your muscles will hurt at first as you push them in ways they haven't been pushed for so long, but it feels great because the pain lets you know that it's working.

It's the same with changing your career and life. Experiencing a bit of discomfort along the way is like the detox from all of the years of feeling numb and miserable. And once you break through those temporary moments of pain, you'll see that on the other side is enjoyment that you've been missing for so long. Just don't let any minor hurdles put you off continuing with the race.

Exercise – Planning for the Future

Once you've been through the processes around your immediate desires and needs, you can start planning for the future by using the personal and business plan which you can find at www.changeyourcareer.org/plan

The plan allows you to plot out a timeline over the next few years (with the period to be adjusted to suit your own personality) which combines figuring out what you want to achieve in your personal life and how your business or work life can help you to do that. For most of us, our work only exists to pay for the things we want to do in our personal lives unless, of course, we manage to reach dream level number 10 and spend our time earning money for the things we love to do.

Has it ever occurred to you that despite how important our lives are we tend not to spend any real time planning out exactly what it is that we want from them? And then we get really frustrated when they haven't turned out as we'd hoped. Maybe that's because we never devoted any real time to think properly about the things we want.

In my experience, having a well thought-through plan is far more likely to lead to you achieving the things you want to achieve in your personal and work life over the coming years.

Going through that process will also allow you to acknowledge the things you simply don't know about yet. For example, until you have employed someone there's no way of knowing whether it's something you will like or not. Employing people is a unique experience that some people enjoy and others hate. At times in my career I have been both of those people, but with everything I've learnt now I think that I'd be happy to be an employer again because I have far more experience of how to be a good one than I had when I first started out when I was, to be frank, absolutely useless as a boss despite my best efforts.

The key here is to figure out the parts of any plan that are unknowns to you. Then, if possible, find someone who has experienced those unknowns and can act as a mentor or a coach. You can learn from them, ask questions and plan for scenarios in advance. Going through that process is also a good way of identifying any gaps in your knowledge, which you can account for and learn as much as possible about before starting.

If you are preparing to start a business, I would recommend highly that you consider writing a culture document that sets out the 'why' of your organisation[3]. You can read the culture document of Netflix by searching 'Netflix culture document' on your favourite search engine. That shows you what one of the biggest and best companies in the world has set out for its own internal rules, although it's worth bearing in mind that your

---

[3]   I'd also recommend reading Start with Why and Find your Why, by Simon Sinek.

version can be much shorter provided that it captures the key points.

A culture document will enable you to identify clearly the key things that you want your business to represent and that will help with things like recruiting people in the future, or working with contractors, because you will be able to provide them a copy and establish at an early stage whether a potential employee or business partner is a good fit for you.

If you are considering starting a business, there are more resources available to help you at *www.changeyourcareer.org/business*

The most important thing is to figure out what you want to do, think through the plan and, most importantly, get started.

"Advertising has us chasing cars and clothes, working jobs we hate so we can buy shit we don't need"

–TYLER DURDEN, FIGHT CLUB

What are you prepared to sacrifice?

Ultimately, having been through everything in this book, how much you want to change at this point in your life might determine which of the things from Chapter 5 you're prepared to move between categories.

Ideally, you want to push as many things down a category as you can.

For example, even with the things you currently have in the essential (non-negotiable) category, which I'd guess might include your rent or mortgage, ask yourself do you really need a house that big in the area in which you live, a car that expensive or all those clothes for you, or your kids, or are each of those things just your ego and insecurity running (and ruining) your life?

If you are desperate to change your life for the better, are you prepared to downsize your house for 12 months or move to a less expensive area to test whether the money you save could help you to build a better life in the medium to long term?

Remember that very few things are permanent. You could rent out the house you live in while renting a less expensive house in a different area to give you the head room in your budget to at least try to make changes, or decide not to buy any new clothes for the next 12 months other than in an emergency, always asking yourself what's the worst that could happen. Usually the answer to that question is 'not much' and you can reverse whatever decision you made if you need to.

Using the house example, if you rented out your house for 12 months to halve your mortgage and things didn't work out, you could just move back in at the end of that period and it would be like nothing ever happened, except you'll have the peace of mind of knowing that you gave something else a try so that it's not playing on your mind anymore.

Often just trying out the grass on the other side is enough to remind us that the grass we live on is pretty good after all, so a temporary experiment can be worthwhile if only to make you more grateful for the things you've been taking for granted.

As long as you weren't reckless during your test period you may be surprised how easily you can go back to what you were doing before if you really want to.

Bear in mind that whatever you are currently doing has led you to being so unhappy that you bought this book and no doubt others like it, so continuing on the same path is unlikely to make you any happier and is unlikely to solve your problems. As the famous line goes, the definition of insanity is doing the same thing over and over and expecting different results.

So, maybe it's finally time to try something new after you've noted one last warning.

The Illusion of Choice

There's a quirk of psychology that is a potential trap for you when you start to consider changing careers, which I want to highlight in case it's not obvious from the work we've already done together. I have fallen into this trap in the past and have seen countless others do the same, because it wasn't clear that it was even a threat.

Have you ever been offered a selection of options to choose from, and found yourself picking something that you later regretted? Think of it as a bit like when a magician asks you to take a card from a deck. It appears on the surface as though you have freedom of choice, but something in the back of your mind tells you that it wasn't free choice at all.

Beware the same issue when it comes to selecting your next career.

Often, we find ourselves choosing from options that are presented to us rather than something we actually, purposefully selected. You might be unsettled in your job and another offer comes along which you then consider, weighing up its pros and cons before deciding whether or not to accept it. Maybe you'll get lucky and get more than one option appear at the same time, giving you the illusion of choice.

Don't fall for it.

The whole purpose of this book is to help you to select what you want to do next in your life based on a careful analysis of what you enjoy doing on a daily basis, what you dislike doing and what fits in with your wants and needs. After going through that process and determining what type of role fits the bill, if you happen to be offered something that meets your criteria you are almost certainly in tune with the universe and shouldn't hesitate to jump on it.

But don't make the mistake of accepting something just because it seems like it might be a bit better than what you're currently doing if it doesn't meet the criteria that you've worked so hard to figure out.

Turning down opportunities that will not make you considerably happier in the next phase of your life is just as important, if not more important, than selecting something that you think will take you to where you want to be.

So, whenever an opportunity comes along check it against your set criteria and, if it doesn't tick the vast majority of your requirements, keep searching for a role or opportunity that does. A new offer can serve as a great catalyst for change without being something that you have to accept.

Once you've checked all of this off your list, the only thing left to do is to get started.

"I've got no car and it's breaking my heart, but I've found a driver and that's a start"

8

SECRET 6
TAKING FIRST STEPS

Have you heard of The Beatles?

If you answered 'no' to that I might have to demand that you return the book.

Where I'm from they tell you about The Beatles in the hospital just after you're born, to make sure that you can always identify yourself properly when speaking to new people.

I remember when I first started traveling abroad when I was younger, chatting to people from other countries and, when they asked where I was from, I would reply on autopilot with *"I'm from Liverpool, you know, where The Beatles are from"*.

Nine times out of 10 it would result in at the very least an understanding of where that was and, often, an excited exchange about one of the most famous bands of all time.

I'm a fan. Not a super fan, but someone who likes a fair amount of their songs and still has spells listening to them when I'm in a certain mood. I once pretended to be John Lennon's long lost son to some girls on holiday when I was 17, but that's another story for another day.

Of all of the many Beatles songs that I love, *Drive My Car* has become one of my favourite songs the older I've grown despite not being on my radar when I was a kid.

I'll tell you why.

If you don't already know, the song is about a boy that meets a girl who wants to be a movie star. She tells him that he can be her driver and, instead of working for peanuts, he can work for her and she'll show him a good time.

He's in. What an offer. Driving a girl around who's going to be a star of the big screen? It would have sounded good to me in my younger days.

He tells her he can start right away and she says, *"Listen babe I've got something to say. I've got no car and it's breaking my heart, but I've found a driver and that's a start."*

I often think of that line. It's beautiful and absolutely perfect for where you are right now.

You see, most people might think that to be a movie star you need to start by focusing on becoming a movie star then think about getting a driver afterwards.

I've learned that isn't necessarily true.

When I was weighing up my options at the second large law firm I worked at, they told me that if I worked hard for the next 10 years I'd be made partner and the rewards would be great. I did some quick maths and figured out that if I worked for them for

10 years, I would probably make over five million pounds for the firm while picking up around one tenth of that in salary. And I'd still be reliant on someone else deciding whether I could be called a partner after all that.

I realised if I continued working for someone else's law firm, ultimately, I wouldn't be in control of when I was made a partner. The standard way to become a partner is to just keep trying to be one for as long as it takes for the existing partners to deem you worthy of promotion.

But I realised that if I set up my own law firm then I'd become one immediately.

So, that's what I did. I figured out how to start a law firm, called myself managing partner of a one-person business and, boom, everywhere I went suddenly I was a partner. I'd go to an event and I'd be sitting on the partners' table and, after only a few months, the partners in other firms started talking to me as one of their peers.

I skipped about nine years of frustration. The system told me that to be a partner I needed to work in the pre-set structure for a decade playing by their rules, but I decided to make my own rules.

I believe that you need to walk the walk of whatever you want to be in life for people to believe that's what you are. Not 'faking it 'til you make it', but actually being the thing you want to be before society tells you that you can be it.

It's being a movie star by acting like a movie star first, not waiting for someone else to tell you that you are one. It's finding the driver before getting the car, because it's inevitable that you'll get the car anyway, so you might as well find a driver now.

And that's one of the general secrets to life. Most people think that you need the world to accept that you are able to do the thing you want to do before you start doing it, but that's nonsense. If that were true, no one would ever be able to do something for the first time because the world wouldn't believe that they could do it without prior proof.

Just think about that for a second. Richard Branson would never have been able to start a music store, or a train company or any one of the many businesses he set up, because before he started them he didn't know anything about them and the world would have said he didn't know what he was doing.

Elon Musk would never have started making electric cars or building spaceships, and Mark Zuckerberg would never have started Facebook.

But they did. They just got on with it and, once they had shown everyone that they could do what they said they could, everyone got on board and never questioned it again.

That's how the world works, you just need to get started. The big issue that I find with most people at this point is that they're scared of taking a leap of faith.

Is that you? Are you scared of jumping off a cliff?

Don't be.

I see all the time lately people talking about a fear of taking a leap or a big jump, usually when it comes to making some big change in their life, business or career.

I know that most people and lots of books like this one are telling you to just do it anyway. Just make that jump or take the leap. They'll tell you things like *"feel the fear and do it anyway"*.

But the first thing I always think when I hear those words is how frightening they sound.

Of course you don't want to jump off a cliff, why would you? Unless you're an experienced cliff jumper, there's nothing much to gain from jumping off cliffs, and I definitely wouldn't recommend it. Despite having walked over the top of the Sydney Harbour Bridge, I wouldn't be keen to jump off a cliff, especially in relation to business, and I've already started three businesses before now. The more I learn about business, the more I realise that far from being the biggest risk takers, the greatest entrepreneurs in the world are experts at de-risking any opportunity that is presented to them.

So, instead of jumping off a cliff, why not just walk slowly down the stairs to get to the same place?

Use my very catchy and definitely trademarked *"can I tile a bathroom"* theory and you'll find that your goal isn't as big and frightening as you think. It just needs to be broken down into little, achievable pieces that you're confident you can do.

Don't leap when you can take small steps one after the other instead. It's much less likely to lead to a catastrophic outcome and much more likely to get you to where you want to be, one small step at a time.

All of that means you just need to decide which is the first step you're going to take, remembering like the girl in the song that it doesn't necessarily have to be the first step that other people might think of. The most important thing is just to get started and go from there. Start building some momentum and you'll be amazed how far it will take you when it starts gathering pace and you begin to get more and more excited about it.

I'd recommend doing whatever step first you feel most excited by or whichever one is the easiest to achieve. If you're starting your own business, that might mean getting a logo designed so that it starts to become a real thing in your mind that you can start attaching real feelings and plans to.

If you're looking for a new job in a new industry, it might be as simple as contacting relevant recruiters or getting your CV reviewed by a professional CV writer to make sure it reflects just how good you are and isn't 20 years old. Or if you're writing your first kids' book, just focus on writing the first page or the first chapter without worrying about anything else.

There is a list of resources at www.changeyourcareer.org/resources that can help you depending on what you want to do next.

The most important thing of all, though, is just to get started. Don't read this book, feel optimistic about the future then let the momentum drift away.

Once you've made the decision to get started, there's one other factor that, in my experience, seems to cripple lots of people.

Perfectionism

Oh, how I hate perfectionism.

I'm like one of those people who used to smoke and now is a rabid, anti-smoking warlord frowning at every smoker in the world.

I was raised to be a perfectionist. I'm not sure why because neither of my parents are. Maybe they just thought that it would be good for me. I remember coming in from school, delighted that I'd got 95 per cent in a test, to be greeted with a smile and the immortal line, *"Well done, son, but what happened to the other 5 per cent?"*.

In one way it spurred me on to always want to do more and be better so I don't blame them for it, they meant well after all and it was said with a smile and with the best intentions. But, for the most part, what it led to was me never being satisfied with anything. Never being content with life or generally okay with anything. It always needed to be better, always needed to be more. More money, more drink, more attention. More, more, more.

But never happy.

It's a curse on our society and leads, at best, to people being stuck in what they're doing for fear of trying something new and not being able to do it perfectly and, at worst, to depression.

I'm here to tell you as a reformed perfectionist that perfection does not exist. It's a concept created in the minds of lunatics to torture people in their daily lives. You might have heard the line that good is the enemy of great, which is true. If you settle for good you'll never be great but, here's the kicker, if you allow perfection to stop you in your tracks before you even get started, you'll never even make it to good, let alone great.

So, the aim is this. Just get it going. Get started and don't worry about things being perfect because they never are. Think about some of the biggest, most powerful people and companies in the world. Are they perfect? When Apple releases its latest operating system, it has bugs in it every single time. The Amazon website experiences problems and governments cannot run countries to save their lives. Presidents and Prime Ministers can be absolutely useless and they've made it to the very top of their chosen professions, voted for by millions of people while others think that they're incompetent.

Stop looking at others and thinking that they're perfect so you can't compete. You can. Just let go of the idea of perfection being a good thing.

To give you a brilliant example based on this book, as I was preparing to write it I listened to an audiobook in which the author said it took him 18 months to write his paperback. A year and a half. And he's a famous multi-millionaire with hundreds of thousands of followers online.

It took me four days to produce my first draft and a few months from start to finish. The content was gathered over 38 years of life but the writing itself took a matter of weeks.

That would not have been possible if I was aiming for perfection. But I wasn't. I was aiming to produce a book containing as much of my experience as it possibly could, to give you as much value as I possibly could, without delaying any longer than necessary. I have no expectation that this book will be perfect. Far more accomplished authors and business people than me have published books that were not perfect.

I often think back to when I read one of my favourite books of all time, *Start With Why* by Simon Sinek. If you haven't read it I would recommend it highly. Despite its brilliance, though, I got to the end and while completely understanding the reasons for starting with 'why', I had no idea how to find what my 'why' actually was.

It turns out lots of other people had the same issue, which led to a follow up book, *Find Your Why*, being released a few years later.

Nobody is perfect. I could spend 10 years writing this book and you could pick it up and find a typo in the first chapter that I'd become blind to, or there might still be something that doesn't make sense to you or you'd prefer to have more information about.

That is why I'm giving out my email address for any follow-up questions and providing access to a free group in which you can discuss any challenges that you face having read the book (which I explain more in chapter 9), and to which I can provide updates over the coming months and years as I learn new things that I'd like to share with you.

I'm sure that some people will read this book and be horrified by the style, hate the grammar, the flow of paragraphs or any number of other things. I'm not a trained writer. I've never studied English Language or Literature at a high level or learnt how to construct sentences properly other than through my own experiences. I'm sure that some people will like what I do, I hope that some people will love it and I know, for certain, that some people will hate it. No matter what we do in life, there are always going to be a range of reactions to it.

Even without any mistakes being made or some people not liking my writing style, I can guarantee that within a week of publishing I will have learnt something new that I could have included. I already know that will happen, but it would still happen if I waited a week longer before letting it go to print. There will always be something new to learn, always something changing. I've been adding things to this very chapter in the week before it was published.

I can still picture my art teacher when I was 15, who I mentioned earlier. I would be painting a picture and playing around with it, never quite happy, never quite satisfied. He would just walk up behind me and say:

"Paul, it's finished."

"But, sir ... " I'd say *"I'm not happy with this bit and I think that bit could be better and ..."*

"Paul, it's finished. Put your paintbrush down. If you keep playing with it you'll ruin it. It's great just the way it is."

So, if you won't listen to me, listen to Mr Power.

I'm beyond trying to be perfect, because perfect doesn't exist. Once you've accepted that, accepted that you have flaws just like everyone else and that's part of what makes you unique, then you'll be free to do whatever you want in life without the fear of criticism. Just be you. You're good enough and don't let anyone tell you otherwise.

If you can't get started, you might need to revisit Secret 4 in Chapter 6 and figure out exactly what it is that you're using as an excuse.

Ultimately, if you really do want to change your life then stop bullshitting yourself and get on with it. On the other hand, if you've been through this entire book and you've realised that you don't want to change anything and you're happy doing what you're doing right now, and that you can transform your life just by altering your attitude to what's good and bad about your current role, then that's great, too. I've got no interest in persuading you to do something that you don't want to do.

At the end of the day, if you'd rather go to work every day, come home and sit on your couch picking your nose while you watch the Kardashians, that's what you should do. Just be happy doing it and stop beating yourself up because you feel the pressure to do something you don't really want to.

If you want to do it, do it. If you don't, don't. Just stop justifying the things you haven't done with bullshit. If you really want to do it, you will.

If you do want to make a start, do yourself a favour and go and get your driver signed up now, then prepare yourself for the final secret.

The secret of secrets.

9

SECRET 7
SECRET OF SECRETS

"When you grow up, you tend to get told the world is the way that it is, and your life is just to live your life inside the world and try not to bash into the walls too much. But that's a very limited life. Life can be much broader once you discover one simple fact. And that is that everything around you that you call life, was made up by people that are no smarter than you. And you can change it. You can influence it. You can build your own things that other people can use. To shake off this erroneous notion that life is just there, and you're just gonna live in it, versus embrace it. Change it, improve it. Make your mark upon it. And once you learn that, you'll never be the same again."

*   *   *

> *"Here's to the crazy ones. The misfits, the rebels, the*
> *troublemakers, the round pegs in the square holes,*
> *the ones who see things differently. They're not fond of*
> *rules, and they have no respect for the status quo. You*
> *can quote them, disagree with them, glorify or vilify*
> *them. About the only thing you can't do is ignore them.*
> *Because they change things – they push the human race*
> *forward. And while some may see them as the crazy*
> *ones, we see genius. Because the people who are crazy*
> *enough to think they can change the world, are the*
> *ones who do."*
>
> –STEVE JOBS

I'll level with you. There's really no need for this to be a separate chapter, I could have just put this information at the end of the last chapter.

But then there wouldn't be seven secrets, I wouldn't have the letter 'S' for the end of the word "secrets" in the acronym that I used at the start of the book and I would have had to call this whole thing something else, which would have meant a completely different marketing campaign that didn't take advantage of the number of people searching for the term *"career change"* in the world.

So, here's the real secret. There aren't seven secrets. There also aren't *Seven Habits Of Highly Effective People*, despite what Steven Covey said, and *The 4-Hour Work Week* isn't about working four hours a week.

There are just principles, tools, techniques and age-old philosophies that, if you follow, will inevitably lead to you having a fulfilling career and a happier life.

Everything else is just packaging. *Seven Habits Of Highly Effective People* just sounds better than *A Few Ways To Get Better*. The number seven is attractive to lots of people psychologically and the way in which the title rolls off the tongue means it's likely to sell more copies and help more people to make changes to their lives that they might otherwise not make. It's not a coincidence that there are seven secrets in this book.

And there's something really important in that message, which is the real reason for highlighting the point.

It's really easy for each of us to underestimate what we can do and overestimate what everyone else can do. The reality is that you're reading a book that I wrote, but I'm no different to you. I have fears, insecurities and ego running around in my life as well. I face the same challenges as you every day, as does every human on the planet. We are all unique but we aren't different, and that's really important to remember.

I've spent so many years thinking of myself as different to everyone else, and all it did was make me lonely and unhappy. But I've realised lately that I'm not different, and being unique or special in our own ways doesn't inevitably mean that we are also alone. There is no one on the planet who is exactly the same as you. No one else has had your exact experiences, read all of the same books, watched all of the same films or met all of the same people. Even the people closest to you have had lives completely different to yours.

But the same basic things bind us. The core human needs apply to us all and connect us in ways we might not see but are there if we want to find them.

Think of it like this.

For me to have written this book and for you to have read it means that we are connected. We might have never met but we have shared experiences and pain that brings us together. And the same applies to everyone else who reads this. I always felt like I was in the wrong tribe, that I was surrounded by people who didn't understand me and who didn't want the same type of life as I did. While that is true to some extent, it doesn't mean that I don't also share the same basic human needs as all of those people, although it does mean that to feel completely at ease in the world it's important that we connect with others who have the same values, hopes and dreams as us.

Which is why I'm building a tribe of my own.

If having read this you feel that you'd like to connect with more people in the same position as you, with whom you can share your experiences, discuss your problems and inspire each other to achieve more, just head to www.changeyourcareer.org/tribe and let me know. It's completely free to be a part of the community.

The purpose of the tribe is to help you and everyone else in it to live a happier and fulfilling life, and to help change the world one person at a time along the way. If that sounds like something that would add value to your journey, jump over there now and sign up with only your name and email address (no sensitive data required).

You might have heard that you are the average of the five people you spend the most time with. I used to wonder how I could meet more people who wanted the same things as I did in life, before I realised that the people I spend the most time with are authors of books and podcast hosts who talk about all of the things I'm interested in.

I spend far more time with the likes of Tim Ferriss, Gary Vee and Tony Robbins than I ever do with anyone in real life, as you have probably already guessed. So, regardless of who your current five person average is made up of, I want to help you to add more people to your life who can help and support you to make the changes that you want to make.

After all, at the moment you are probably living in a mad house in which the inhabitants do not know that they are mad, so when you tell them about wanting to change your life they're likely to tell you that *you* are the mad one and you shouldn't change. The beauty of finding more sane people is that they will do the complete opposite. They will encourage you to make the difficult decisions necessary to transform your career and your life.

I can say from my own experience that the single biggest factor that I believe separates people who make significant progress in anything from those who delay, procrastinate or never move forward at all, is being accountable to someone or something external to himself or herself. Whether that's a group of people who become accountability partners or using formal coaches, external accountability is crucial for continued success.

I believe that so much that, at the time of writing, I have four coaches in different areas of my life, making sure that I am accountable for the targets I set and goals that I want to achieve from my mental and physical health to general business and specific internet marketing goals.

To illustrate the point, when I trained for a marathon in 2017 I realised about five or six weeks into the training that if I hadn't been part of a wider group meeting every Sunday to do our main training run with our personal trainer and coach, and if I hadn't announced the fact that I was running a marathon to all of my friends and family, I would never have gone through with it. I would have just quit as soon as it got tough and as soon as the weather started turning against us during our 6am runs.

But by having the external accountability and, most importantly, an experienced coach and mentor who provided the perfect blend of inspiration, accountability and a good kick up my arse when I needed it, not only did it force me to carry on when times were tough but it drove me forward to a point where not only was I accepting the challenges that came my way, but I was actively asking the world to throw more at me.

I remember vividly during a 21-mile training run along the coast in gale force winds listening to the artist Pitbull talking about teaching the kids in the schools he's built. They teach that being able to take what life throws at you isn't enough; that you won't be truly successful until you not only take what it throws at you but you ask the planet if that's all it's got. I found myself running the last two miles of that 21-mile run turning into a gale force head wind laughing to myself as I asked the world if that's all it had because I could take more and still move forward. I felt unbeatable again.

From the depths of despair I had battled back, time after time, to take on the world and to ask if that's all it had. Screaming into the wind, demanding more and laughing as I completed the last mile.

The beauty is that once you've started the journey in one area of your life, the results will flow into all of the other parts as well.

I've packaged this as a book about changing your career, but you might have realised it has the potential to be much, much more than that. If you go through each exercise focusing on your life in general rather than just your job you'll uncover hidden challenges that you never knew existed, which will lead to great epiphanies and wonderful breakthroughs that will change your life forever.

I used your career as a gateway drug because there are more people who believe that they can change their jobs than there are people who think that they can change their entire lives. I wanted to tempt you onto the path, hoping that once you've seen what it can do for your working day, you'll believe that it can change your entire existence.

After embarking on your first quest and experiencing the benefits, you will have the desire and belief to continue on multiple adventures for the rest of your life. I feel as though I've finally discovered the secrets of living a happy, stress free work life and, for the first time in as long as I can remember, I feel content and at peace with the world. I feel as though I have recaptured something I lost a long time ago, something that had been dying inside me since I was a little boy.

Maybe something has been dying inside you, too, and maybe, just maybe, it's time to bring it back to life.

As for your current expedition, I know that you have that strength in you to achieve anything you want. Whatever has happened before now, wherever you've been and however hard the world has smacked you down, you've still had the courage and desire to try again. To push another time to make changes that will transform your career and change your life.

Just by doing that you are ahead of 99 per cent of the population, and you should never forget that. Never allow your insecurities to convince you that you aren't worthy of a better life or that 'keeping down with the Joneses' is for you. You are unique, you are special, but you're not different and you're not alone. There are thousands of us out there, all striving for a better way of life, all battling to create better futures for ourselves, our loved ones and our future generations.

The way it has been doesn't need to be the way it always is. It's time. Time to make changes. Time to take a deep breath, to sit up tall, to allow your heart rate to slowly increase as you prepare to charge. For your shoulders to relax and the tension to ease from across your face. For your jaw to move freely, for the energy to begin surging through your body and the hairs on the back of your neck to stand up.

It's time for you to feel the blood pumping through your veins like it hasn't pumped for years, to flood every organ and every cell in your body with oxygen and to feel revitalised. Time to focus, for everything you've read to fix in your mind and all of your hopes and dreams to come to the surface ready to be fulfilled in a way greater than you ever thought possible.

There might be some pain along the way, but I promise you on the other side of that pain is greater joy, love and happiness than you ever could have imagined.

It's time to change your life. It's time to claim what is rightfully yours.

Come and join me in the world of misfits.

Paul Cope
Liverpool, January 2019

THANK YOU

When I decided to write this book, I had no idea how much I would enjoy the process and how excited and intrigued I would be to see whether anyone actually wanted to read the finished product.

It means the world to me that you have taken the time out of your busy schedule to read it, so I wanted to take the time to say thank you. I hope your time and commitment have been repaid, and you've taken something from the preceding pages that has helped you at least in some small way.

Regardless of whether you thought the book was good, bad or indifferent, if you bought it online I would be eternally grateful if you could leave an honest review of it on whatever platform you bought it from. As it's my first book and I would like to write more in the future, any feedback you can give by way of a review will help me and will help others who might be thinking of buying it.

If the book helped you in any way and you think it could help someone you know, please feel free to pass it on to them, and if you have any questions at all about any of the things you've read in the previous pages or if you would like any further guidance or advice, please send an email to me at *paul@changeyour career.org*

I'd also love to hear your views via social media, even if it's just to say that you agree that we should stop referring to bland things as being vanilla.

In fact, that might be my next book.

Thanks again,

Made in the USA
Coppell, TX
11 September 2022